Osage County Kids

To Tami
Love & laughter
Lou Dean 12/99

Lou Dean

CLINESCOT
PUBLISHING
COLORADO

Osage County Kids

Library of Congress Catalog Card Number:
99-94885

ISBN: 0-9671208-2-9

Printed in the United States of America

First Edition September 1999
10 9 8 7 6 5 4 3 2 1

Cover design by Lee Kilmer

CLINESCOT
PUBLISHING
COLORADO

Blue Mountain Road
Dinosaur, Colorado 81610

Dedicated to

BUB

John Phillip Jacobs

He was pulled out of the river one afternoon and brought home in what he described as a "limp and unpromising condition." After restoring him to activity with mullein tea and other remedies, his mother said, "I guess he wasn't in too much danger. People born to be hanged are safe in water."

The Biography of Mark Twain
By Albert Bigelow Pain

I

"Dad," Bub said one evening at supper. "That new rooster of yours is mean. He chases us kids every time we get in the barnyard."

My father gave a half-grin. "Ahh, he won't hurt you. He's supposed to have spirit, he's a fighting cock."

"But lookey here," Bub said, lifting his overalls leg and displaying a half-inch gash. "He spurred me just yesterday when ..."

"That little scratch?" Dad said, in a condescending tone.

After everyone else was sound asleep that night, my terrier dog, Shorty, scratched beneath my bedroom window, as always. I looked over at my older sister rolled beneath her covers and listened for her even breathing, then I unlatched the screen and slipped out, dragging a worn quilt behind.

Shorty and I had just snuggled into a comfortable lump on the creek bank when my brother startled me in the quiet darkness.

"Sissy, we need to talk." Bub said.

Shorty bristled under the quilt and popped his head out. A barely audible growl came from deep in his belly.

"It's just me, Shorty," Bub said, extending his hand. Bub plopped down beside us and in the bright moonlight I watched as he rubbed salve on his wounded ankle. "Sissy, it's up to us to change that rooster's attitude and I know just how we can do it."

Bub had an irritating way of including me without first asking if I'd help. I considered the possible consequence of hurting Dad's prize rooster, then thought of the flashing red-orange blur that terrorized me every time I got near the barn. When I didn't respond, my brother nodded and stood.

"OK, tomorrow then."

"Bub comes up with some excellent schemes," I whispered to my dog as my brother's shadow disappeared across the yard. "But somehow things usually turn around so that I end up in a mess of trouble."

Shorty agreed with an "errf" and then settled warmly against my neck.

Late the next afternoon, when Dad left to go to work on his railroad job, Bub found Shorty and me near the creek catching tadpoles.

My older brother came dragging two dusty gunnysacks and he had our baby brother by the hand.

"This is what we'll do," Bub said, walking toward the barn and motioning for me to follow. "Lil Bub here will meander across the barnyard, lookin real innocent. We'll stay by the corral fence with our sacks." He handed me a gunnysack. "One of us on one side and one on the other. When that darned rooster starts after Lil Bub, we'll throw our sacks over him."

"Then what?" I asked, looking squarely at my big brother. The thought of having that mean rooster in my two hands didn't particularly appeal to me.

"Well ... well, I don't know, exactly. But we'll just torment him. Give him a dose of his own medicine so he'll leave us be."

It didn't sound like an airtight plan to me, but I couldn't think of anything better, so I agreed.

A few minutes later, I hid behind the splintered fence, with my sack held tightly in two sweaty hands. My eyes were glued to the barnyard and Lil Bub's red head. My poor younger brother strutted around, happy to be included in our conspiracy, and completely unaware that he was the bait in a dangerous game.

In a flash it happened. The streak of feathers appeared out of nowhere. I chanced one quick look at Bub and he encouraged me with a wave of his hand. Just as the rooster made his first dive toward Lil Bub, I slid under the fence on hands and knees, tossing my sack.

I had the rooster. He fought and jumped as I frantically held him beneath my sack.

"The water tank," Bub screamed. "Toss him in the tank, Sissy."

Holding onto the fighting rooster was like holding onto a young pig. He flopped and jumped and squalled beneath the sack until my arms began to ache. Bub's words came again.

"Run backwards, toss em in the tank. That'll take the life out of em."

The water tank was just two steps behind me and I had to do something. With all my strength, I scooped the wild sack into my arms, ran backwards and splashed the rooster, sack and all, into the tank.

"Hold em. Keep em down," Bub instructed, running toward me.

The fighting cock continued the struggle, splashing water into my eyes and causing me to spit for breath. I pushed him down harder, sinking my arms deeper until I was up to my neck.

"Get em, Sissy," Lil Bub's shrill voice squealed.

"Hold em. You got em now," Bub encouraged.

Suddenly I felt a difference in my struggle. Nothing was fighting back. The wet sack floated slowly to the surface and one orange leg stuck stiffly out of the water.

"Get em out! Hurry!" Bub was beside me then. Grabbing the sack, he flung the mess of wet feathers and dripping burlap into the dust beside the tank.

All of us stood in silence, staring. Bub gently pulled the bag away from the damp feathers so that a red eye glared at us, fixed and horrid.

"On no," I gasped. "I killed em." I'd never killed a living creature in my life. In the silence that followed Grandma Carrie's voice echoed in my ears. *"Thou shall not kill."*

"Serves him right," Bub said. "Chasin us ever day in our own barnyard."

"Yeah," Lil Bub said. "Serves em right."

"I didn't aim to kill em," I choked. "I've done murder, Bub."

My brother laughed. "I don't think this counts, Sissy. I bet even God likes fried chicken." Bub looked over his shoulder toward the house. "Well, we better bury him deep and far and take an oath never to breathe a word of this or Dad will strap us sure."

My eyes were still fixed on the wet mess of feathers and stiff orange legs, but I managed a nod. Then, my heart stopped. I stared in disbelief. One of the stiff claws drew up ever so slightly. "He moved," I screamed. "Look! He's still alive."

The rooster blinked a red eye, stiffened, quivered, then jumped to his feet. He gave us all one quick stare then took off at a dead run.

Bub commenced hollering with laughter and Lil Bub joined in. I couldn't manage an outright giggle, but my heart was singing. I hadn't killed Dad's rooster.

About a week later Dad mentioned the personality change in his rooster. We were calmly eating breakfast and I'd just packed my jaws with a huge bite of honey-soaked corn cake.

"That damned game rooster of mine is acting crazy. Runs ever time I get near him."

I drew in a deep breath and the wad of food hung in my throat. Bub pounded me on the back until I finally drew air.

Dad's eyes narrowed and he glared at me with a suspicious glance. I softened my face into a tender look of complete innocence, with eyebrows raised, mouth slightly open. It was a look I later learned to practice in the mirror.

"You kids been messing with my rooster?" The words cracked out like a whip.

"No sir," came the trio.

Sis wasn't a part of the sin. She turned her head very slowly toward me and Bub and her eyes sparkled with amused disbelief. It was all I could do to keep a smile from fluttering. My older sister knew we were lying and I knew she knew.

"Well," Dad squalled after a moment of strained silence. "I don't know what in hell has gotten into that rooster. If you get within fifty feet of him, he turns and runs like a damned rabbit." Dad took a sip of coffee and a grin played at one corner of his mouth. "Was gonna name him McCowan after the old boy who gave him to me. Guess I better make it McCoward."

My lips twitched as I fought the urge, but Bub and Lil Bub chuckled. The three of us gradually merged into Dad's joke with great enthusiasm. He seemed pleased at our reaction.

My older brother who loved reading the wit of Will Rogers, was practicing to be a philosopher. He joined me on the creek that night just as Shorty and I snuggled into our quilt.

"When I hear someone make the comment that people don't change, I take issue with that," he said, putting a straw between his lips. "Our friend, McCowan, for instance. Personalities can change, depending on circumstance and motivation."

II

Carolyn Ann White moved on the farm just north of us when I was eight and quickly became like a sister to me. At school we loved to draw pictures and make up stories of what we'd do when we grew up. Afternoons, as soon as homework and chores were done, we'd scurry to our hideout beneath the bridge that bordered our two farms. The creek that trickled over the floor of our bridge, became a wonderland for us. We spent hours playing with the assortment of fishes, frogs, crawdads, and dragonflies that were our neighbors.

Being my sister was, at times, a mixed blessing. The packaged deal included a hormone-driven big sister, a baby brother who tagged along, an older brother who loved to torment, a stoic father who inflicted harsh punishments, and a "here-again-gone-again Mama."

One particular fine day in the summer of 1958, Carolyn and I had set to work building ourselves a lean-to against a giant cottonwood behind the barn near the creek. We'd worked for hours propping limbs against the tree, forming a half tepee, covering our new home with leafy branches until the result pleased us.

We then decided to play Tarzan and Jane and, after drawing straws, took our proper places. We had to draw straws to see who was unfortunate enough to play Jane, because Tarzan got to do all the fun stuff. He swung across the creek on the grapevines letting out great bursts of enthusiastic squalls to announce his arrival. He hunted with bow and arrow and spear, displaying his pretend game with great pride, then he sat comfortably inside his home while Jane made tea and mud pies and busied around the house in womanly fashion, her bark skirts switching.

Just as we had decorated ourselves in finery of bark clothing, mud masks and cottonwood bobbles, set up our plan, and begun to get in the midst of our game, my brother stuck his head into our house.

"You call this a hideout? Lil Bub could build something better than this. Why, Grandma could outdo it." He gave our house a push and to my dismay, the entire morning's work squeaked, tilted and went crashing to the ground.

Shorty, who had been transformed into Tarzan's pet chimp, Cheetah, barked frantically when the structure of limbs and leaves crashed down on him. I dived into the crumple and rescued my dog who was tied to the base of the tree. Shorty dearly loved to play along with Carolyn and me, but when it came to playing Cheetah, he would try to run off and hide. I think he was insulted at being made into a monkey. He would sit stoically during the entire game and refuse the "stick" bananas we offered with a look of pure disgust.

"You jackass," I spit, reaching for Bub. "You almost killed my dog. Leave us alone. We don't need your stupid opinion."

In his usual style, my brother dodged my attack, cut himself a thick stump of grapevine, stuck it in his mouth, and proceeded to intrude. Pulling a match from his shirt pocket, Bub lifted his leg. Jerking the stick across his tight breeches, he gave a little smirk when it sparked, then he lit the grapevine. Stepping up on the heap of sticks that had been our house, he drew in a slow drag of smoke and pushed out fascinating little rings.

"You two want to build a real hideout? We're talkin secret place. A genuine Army dugout, a foxhole. Something no one in the entire world could ever find."

He added intrigue by the motions of his free hand and the rise and fall of his voice. Carolyn looked at me. Inheriting a brother like Bub had its merit. At school no one could look at us crossways or Bub would whip them. He endeared himself in other little ways sometimes too, by surprising us with a can of cold pop or sharing a candy bar he'd traded someone out of.

"Where would we build such a grand hideout?" Carolyn asked. "Probably have to go to the far end of the farm nearly to the Arkansas River."

"Not true," Bub said, quickly taking advantage of the hint of interest. "Right here beneath your nose, within spittin distance. A place where even Dad will walk right over it and not see a thing."

Carolyn and I looked at each other, intrigued.

"Walk right OVER it?" I asked.

The scene was set, and my brother was satisfied completely as he relaxed on the creek bank while Carolyn and I went to the shop to collect shovels, buckets, and a piece of tin.

"Cut carefully now," Bub towered over Carolyn and me as we worked on our knees. "The sod must come out in nice, neat squares."

"Why?" I asked, irritated that my morning's play with my friend had somehow turned into one of Bub's personal expeditions.

"Don't doubt the expert, Sissy," Bub said, knocking ashes from his grapevine. "Just work."

I cast a squinted glance toward my older brother. Clad in faded jeans and T-shirt, his cotton hair shucked out from his cap like silk beneath a corn husk. "Don't push your luck, Bub."

He didn't comment or seem to react, but I saw the slightest flicker of his lips as he chewed on the grapevine. He was enjoying himself completely.

An hour later, I trudged toward the creek with a heaping bucket of red clay. I emptied my burden, straightened my back, and winced when a burning pain shot up between my shoulder blades.

"I can't believe he talked us into this," I said, as Carolyn dumped her bucket. "We were having this perfectly fine time and here comes my brother and now we're slaves."

"It'll be grand when we're finished, Sissy. Just wait and see. And we'll have it forever. Our own special place that no one knows about. Just think of it. We can hide from the entire world."

My friend echoed all of the promises Bub had recited the past three hours as we worked. I tried to find a peace with the plan, but somewhere in the deepest part of me, a struggle was taking place.

"All I know is, Bub took a perfectly good Saturday morning and turned it into work. And ... you haven't had him for a brother as long as I have. His great plans backfire. He's famous for gettin me in trouble ..."

"Let's move along, girls. What's the delay over there?"

"If you want it to move faster, get a shovel and bucket in your hands," I said, giving Bub a despicable look as we walked toward him.

"You'd never make it in the military, Sissy. Can't submit to authority."

That did it. I threw my bucket to the ground and spit. "And I suppose by 'AUTHORITY' you would be referrin to yourself?"

"Certainly. I'm in command. The boss. The one in charge. Your supervisor."

I stretched myself up into Bub's face and sneered. "Eat dirt."

Like a flash, Bub wrestled me to the ground and we rolled and tumbled until he had me pinned, my arms flat against the grass.

Shorty, who'd been helping with the dirt digging, jumped around us with excited "errfs" and nipped at Bub's feet. Released from his humiliating position as Cheetah, he was ready to defend my honor at any cost.

"Now, Sissy dear, perhaps you'd like to change your attitude? Some of us are meant to be leaders, others followers."

I squirmed and cursed, but Bub held me while my dog continued to bark. "I know about followin you. It can lead to a whole mess of trouble."

Bub ignored my words completely. "After all, you've done this hard work and we're nearly finished. Why quit now?"

Carolyn, who'd stopped long enough to watch the wrestling match agreed from the hole. "It's true, Sissy. Look. The hideout is almost to my neck. We can't stop now."

Bub raised an eyebrow in question and I gave a reluctant nod of my head. "OK, but shut the orders, Bub. I mean it."

My brother let me up, handed me a shovel, and proceeded to brush dirt from his jeans. "Shorty, if you ever really bite me, Buddy, I'm gonna put your lights out." Bub grinned down at my spotted dog.

"Touch my dog and you're history."

That afternoon, after a quick lunch break of peanut butter and honey sandwiches, we resumed our work. Bub finally pitched in, carrying a few buckets of dirt to the creek. When the sun began to fade beneath the pecan trees in the west field, Bub jumped down in the huge hole and invited us in.

There was just room enough for the three of us to squat into the cool darkness. "See, isn't this grand? I told you it would be."

I wasn't that impressed. Something about being in the dugout made me nervous. I much preferred the trees and our lean-to where a person could peer out. "I like windows."

"Hand grenades come through windows, Sissy dear. This is a foxhole. Bulletproof."

Carolyn's enthusiasm had also waned. "We better cover it, cause I gotta get home."

"Yeah, we got chores to do too," I agreed.

Bub used Dad's snip pliers to cut the piece of tin the exact size of the hole. Placing the tin over the hideout, he then began to put the chunks of sod carefully back in place. When he stood, he was genuinely impressed with his own work.

"See, no one could ever guess. Not in a million years."

Even though I didn't agree out loud I had to admit to myself, Bub did a fine job of hiding the foxhole.

"Tomorrow." Bub said the word like a declaration. "Tomorrow I'll fetch Larry Gene. We'll get Lil Bub and have us a great battle right here." He fell down on one knee. "Fourscore and seven years ago, our fathers brought forth on this continent a new nation, conceived in liberty and dedicated to the proposition that all men are created equal."

Carolyn looked at me and grinned. One thing about my brother. He had a way of adding color which somehow eased the discomfort of what he always put you through. He memorized great chunks of oratory and would blurt it out at just the right moment, catching his audience unaware and captivating them.

Standing, he took off his cap and bowed. "Tomorrow then Ladies. At noon, on this great battleground, we will meet again."

Carolyn decided to hang out with me while I fed my chickens. Just as I handed my friend a bucket and we began gathering eggs, I heard the distant sound of Dad's tractor. For some odd reason, he wasn't taking his usual route down the worn path in front of the barn. The realization of that hit me about the same time I heard the peculiar noises.

My father had made the decision to hook onto a dead tree and drag it up to a brush pile near the creek behind the barn. He was driving along slowly, looking back at his cargo, when the front end of the tractor fell five feet into a mysterious hole, ejecting Dad onto the ground like a discarded banana peel. He came up squalling like a panther and began to scream at Bub.

Bub, closest to the fiasco, was feeding his pigs at the time. I'm sure he must have seen the mishap coming. It's my guess he tried out a quick prayer, but God was busy with other things that particular afternoon. How my older brother had the nerve to walk toward Dad I will never know. Had it been me, I'm convinced, I would have disappeared quickly in the opposite direction.

Carolyn and I emerged just as Bub got within Dad's reach. My father jerked Bub up off the ground like a feather, holding him by the front of the shirt. "What in hell's name do you think you're doing digging a God forsaken hole in the middle of the field? Damned hole big enough to bury a cow in!"

Several other sentences I dare not repeat followed as Bub dangled at the end of Dad's arm like a wind chime dancing in the breeze. My brother kept squeaking out little explanations, none of which my father even heard. Finally, Dad dropped Bub to his feet, ordered him to go get the truck, and motioned for Carolyn and me to come.

"You two girls in on this?" The question was a grizzly growl. My father's face was white and his red hair flamed above his sunburned ears.

The first impulse, of course, was to lie. Lying was out of the question. I'd only seen my father that mad a couple of times in my life and I'd learned some things from those two experiences. In these situations Dad had a tendency to go slightly insane. It didn't pay to lie or bother with lame excuses. Taking full responsibility for your actions, although risky, was the only choice.

"Yes sir," I said, feeling my friend quaking beside me.

"Well I'm not even gonna ask how you three kids managed to move a ton of damned dirt in one afternoon or why. But wherever the hell you put it, start bringing it back. This MINUTE."

"Yes sir." I jumped in the direction of the shop to fetch bucket and shovel and Carolyn traveled close beside.

Using a fat chain and the pickup, Bub and Dad finally managed to drag the tractor from the hole, then worked up until dark repairing the radiator. Carolyn and I shoveled the dirt near the creek bank into our buckets and carried it back to the dugout. Just as the sun disappeared in a mess of clouds, Carolyn's dad, Frank, appeared, walking up from the barnyard.

Frank and Dad exchanged a quick conversation then Dad hollered out for Carolyn.

"Reckon I'll see you tomorrow." Carolyn said, dropping the shovel and pushing at the water blisters on her hands.

"I told you about Bub and trouble. One follows the other."

"Well," Carolyn said. "The thing I like about your house, it's never boring over here."

Bub walked up grinning. "Need a hand, Sissy? You might be here most of the night if you didn't have a big strong brother."

Carolyn waved and trotted off as Bub reached for her bucket and shovel.

"Chances are," I said, "If I didn't have a big strong brother, I wouldn't be here at all."

Bub tossed his head back and gave out a fine laugh.

Sis ambled to the back of the barnyard about that time, curiously peering at the scene below. "Suuppperr," she sang out. "Fried chicken and gravy."

My mouth went wet. In that moment I knew what it truly meant to be hungry. I'd done manual labor all day. My muscles ached, my back hurt, and my belly rumbled at the thought of warm food.

"They aren't eating until they finish this little chore," Dad said.

His words sent a dread through me. Everything hurt. The water blisters on my hands, my tired feet, the burning between my shoulders, my aching arms.

It was after midnight when Bub and I carried the last two buckets of dirt up the hill. Bub tramped it down and we both sighed.

"I'll get Dad," Bub said, starting for the house.

I slumped over onto the heap of cool dirt and stretched my weary body.

Our father came with his flashlight and approved with a grunt. For an extended moment we all stood in the darkness of the warm night. Finally Dad cleared his throat. I was half expecting the switch to be next on the agenda, and for once in my life, the thought didn't fill me with fear. I hurt in so many places, what was one more ache?

"My tractor could have been completely obliterated," Dad said. "That would have sent us into financial ruin. Could have lost the wheat and the hay and ... Bub, I swear, if you ever do anything this stupid again, I think I might drown you."

"Yes sir." Bub agreed.

"Go on up to the house the two of you. Sis left chicken and gravy on the stove."

Bub and I filled our plates with warm chicken, bread, and gravy, then headed outside to the picnic table. Every step I took hurt in several places.

I felt Bub's eyes on me as I ripped ravenously into the chicken. In the moonlight I saw his lips stretch into a slow smile.

"Delayed gratification," he said. "One of life's true pleasures."

"Shut up," I said. Shorty lifted his head from my lap and growled. "You'll never live to be a philosopher," I spit through my food. "Shorty says, if Dad doesn't kill you, someone else will."

III

The first night I spent with my new friend, Carolyn, was a cultural shock. Her parents, Cookie and Frank, interacted with each other much differently than my parents. When Mama was home and she and Dad were still struggling to make their marriage work, almost every real conversation they had ended in an argument.

That first time at Carolyn's house, sitting at the supper table, I was nervous. Even though her parents and brother Steve seemed nice enough, being in someone else's home was a new experience for me. The last thing Dad said was, "Mind your manners." My biggest fear was knowing just what those manners were supposed to be and if mine were the same as theirs.

When Frank hit the table with his fist and hollered, "Get me some more tea, Ma," a shudder rattled across my shoulders.

My eyes flashed quickly across the table to Carolyn's mother who seemed to be deaf. She didn't react at all to the command. In fact, she finished buttering her corn bread with several slow motions of the knife and didn't even look Frank's way.

"Bam!" The fist again hit the table. My fingers shook in my lap and for an instant I had an almost irresistible urge to bolt. Instinct said, *"Run! Jump from the table and scurry out the door across the terraces to the safety of your dog and your hiding place beneath the trees."* I knew what anger sounded like and at our house, I knew what usually followed.

This second blast through the silence did get results. Cookie put down her corn bread and turned her head toward her husband with a look of what seemed to be amusement. I watched in complete terror.

"I said I wanted some more tea, Ma. When I say FROG, you jump."

Cookie quickly pushed back her chair and with feet together at the heels, she hopped toward the kitchen croaking, "Rivveet, Rivveet." Carolyn, Steve, and Frank roared with laughter.

It took me several minutes to recover, but when I was able to smile, it was the grandest kind of feeling. The world broadened in that moment and life brightened with new possibilities.

The next morning Carolyn begged for us to have soda pop and peanut butter with toast. The idea danced across my mind like a tumbleweed in the wind, filling me with joy. I had never cared for breakfast foods. Dad was a great advocate of eggs and oatmeal both of which I'd learned to loathe. We had an ongoing battle of the wills over cleaning up every bite of the dreaded bulk every single morning.

My friend's request was met with a giggle from Cookie, who seemed to delight in the idea. She bowed at the waist. "Do let me serve you, ladies."

Then with great ceremony, she seated us outside on the porch and proceeded to bring us bubbly soda pop, hot toast, and peanut butter with honey.

It took only one such day in Frank and Cookie's house to know I'd found a refuge from the storm. Gradually, the White family added several dimensions to my life. Frank became good friends with my dad and when Mama was home, she and Cookie visited, and Steve and Sis became sweethearts.

On moonlit summer nights, Carolyn and I would follow along as Frank trained his coonhounds for the field trials. While Frank laid a trail out over the fields into the woods by dragging a coon hide, Carolyn and I each held a bouncing eager hound on a leash. Then when Frank gave the signal, we released our dogs and ran behind, chasing until our lungs burned to see which dog would be first to the tree and which would bark first.

Many a winter evening I sat curled next to Carolyn on the couch while Frank told stories of their champion field trial dog, Sailor. He'd point to the tall trophies on the mantle and I'd visualize the crowds of people milling around the competitions, the excitement of the chase and what it must feel like to walk away with the trophy, your dog prancing proudly by your side.

My Dad was a daily drinker who loved his home brew. To my knowledge he never missed a day of work from drinking or allowed one thing at the farm to go undone, but he did love to stand around the shop and exchange pleasantries with the neighbor men while he consumed great amounts of "brew."

Frank, on the other hand, was no drinker. Perhaps his half-Indian heritage affected that decision, or his five-foot-three Irish wife.

I only remember Frank and Dad drinking together on one occasion. It was June, the end of wheat harvest, and Steve pulled away in White's old truck with the last load of golden grain heading for the co-op. Dad and Frank settled out in the yard beneath the shade of the great elms and began to drink. Every now and again Dad would whistle at Carolyn and me as we played nearby in the creek. Waving an empty beer bottle over his head, he'd motion for us to bring two more.

The talk between Frank and Dad grew louder and great bursts of laughter became more frequent. Then my Dad stood and began to make his way toward his pickup that was parked near the shop. Frank followed with some effort. Trying to measure his steps, he bumped into the gate which sent him spiraling in a half-stagger toward the truck.

After a few minutes, the old Ford fired and disappeared slowly down the gravel road in a puff of red dust. Carolyn and I had moved from the creek to our tree house when we saw the truck return.

During our fathers' absence we'd decided to introduce our dogs to the tree house. It had taken some doing. Although Shorty was a willing customer for most anything, he began to wiggle in my arms as I climbed the ladder and it took both of us a lot of work to get Fly Boy to cooperate.

While we sat, waiting for our Dads to emerge from the truck, both dogs whined in our arms, wanting down from the tree. Fly Boy kept squirming, trying to jerk out of his collar while Shorty fussed at me with continuous "errfs."

It was quickly apparent that our fathers had somehow continued their celebration. It was Dad now who measured his steps and was making an obvious effort to walk. He took three wobbly strides out of the truck then turned and went back to help his buddy. Poor Frank could barely stand and the two of them made less than half a man as they struggled back toward the picnic table.

When they were finally seated, Dad pulled a pint of whiskey from his overalls' pocket, took a swig, and handed the bottle to Frank. The afternoon progressed that way until they emptied the bottle and Dad motioned for me to fetch them another beer.

"This stuff's green," he said. "Musta batched it too soon. Damn, I hate to pour it all out, waste all that sugar and ..."

"Let's walk down and feed it to the hogs. I'll bet they'll drink it. Hogs eat anything."

Dad's face lit up with a big smile and he slammed Frank on the back. "Let's do it." He sat for a minute looking at the distance between the shop and the barn. "Sissy, you and Carolyn bring those fresh bottles of brew to us at the barnyard."

Frank and Dad made their way slowly down the path that led to the barn and Carolyn and I jingled along behind, each carrying a box of beer bottles.

At the pigpen, Dad uncapped the first quart and poured it into the hog trough. Bub's Chester White sow came grunting up, curious and always ready for food. She stuck her snout deep into the amber liquid and sucked with noisy slurps, stopping once to look up at her audience, blinking her long-lashed eyes. Soon, her weanling piglets joined in, stepping over into the brew, rallying for position in the trough.

"By God, they love it, Frank. Watch em drink that up." Dad opened another bottle and then another, re-filling the trough as the pigs' noisy slobbering broke the afternoon silence.

Carolyn and I perched on the fence and watched as Dad emptied the box of quart bottles one by one in the trough while the pigs sucked up the brew. Within fifteen minutes the circus began. The old sow, heavy with pregnancy, walked a few feet from the trough and dropped in her wallow with a grunt. Then, letting out a long moan of pleasure, she stretched herself out and rolled over on her back, all the while, making cooing noises of contentment. After only a moment, she seemed to remember the source of her newly found pleasure and tried to get up so she could return to the trough.

The sow groaned, struggled to her feet, and began to go in the general direction of the beer. She staggered shamelessly in a great jagged line, bumping into the fence, trailing off into the peach trees, and finally falling to the ground for a short rest.

Carolyn and I remained on top of the fence, watching as our fathers barked outbursts of laughter, pointing and slapping their legs. Soon, they were sharing a quart of the "pig beer," drinking it as though it were the best they'd ever had.

When the red cloud of dust came roaring down the gravel driveway, I nudged Carolyn and pointed. She squinted into the afternoon sun.

"Trouble," she said in a whisper. "That's my mother."

Cookie banged the old blue truck right off the gravel road by the house, made a swing across the low place in the creek and barreled down in front of the barn. Slamming on the brakes she sent a drifting cloud of soft dirt right over us. She reached into the back of the truck and pulled out a broom. Bare feet flying, she quickly covered the distance to the pigpen with a look of quiet determination.

"Frank White, you know how I feel about drinking. You know."

Frank, who by then was too drunk to stand alone, was clinging to the fence, beer bottle in one hand.

"Hi Maa," he slurred and a stupid grin spread across his round face.

With the first swipe of her broom, Cookie took out the bottle in Frank's hand, sending it jutting into the dust, bubbling and belching. The second blow caught Frank somewhere near the shoulders and he grabbed both hands on the fence for support. It was the third hit that finished the job nicely. The broom landed flush against the side of Frank's head, detaching him from the fence. He crashed, face down in the dirt, like a giant tree felled by an axe.

"Dean Jacobs, load him in the truck," Cookie demanded.

Dad didn't hesitate. The attack must have had a sobering effect on him, because he scooped Frank up and with little effort managed to walk his friend toward the White's old pickup where he deposited him in the bed with a "thump."

Dad quickly gathered up the empty beer bottles and made his way slowly toward the shop like a humbled child.

Bub's laughter sounded softly from the hayloft, so Carolyn and I climbed up to join him. "You reckon your Mama will whop on him some more when they get home?" Bub asked, handing us both a stick of gum.

Carolyn carefully unwrapped the gum and stuck it between her jaws, chewing it down to a manageable lump. "No, I reckon not. My mother has a temper, true enough. But it's kind of like a tornado. It's fast and furious, then its gone and the clouds pass and the sun comes out."

IV

Strangers at the farm were a rare and welcome attraction to us kids. When a red cloud of dust appeared on our gravel road, we all usually began to meander toward the front gate. Almost always, if the visitor wasn't a neighbor looking for Dad, it was someone lost.

"Did we pass Ponca City?"

"Is this the road that leads to Fairfax?"

"According to our map, this should take us to Pawhuska, then on over to Tulsa."

Since Dad was always either working in town at his railroad job or in the field, it was a chance for Sis and Bub to be in authority and test their social skills.

If the lost traveler was fortunate, he'd get Sis first at the gate. She had developed a keen sense of place, learning all the road numbers, directions, and distances between local towns. She loved dearly to share her atlas-like skills, taking great pride in her abilities.

"Which direction did you come from? Are you traveling north on this road?" She'd point and the stranger would nod. "Well, you're doing great. You just haven't gone quite far enough. See that school house up there on the hill? Just stay on the road you were on and keep going that way. That's North. Go about a mile past the school. You come to a stop sign. That's Highway 60. Hang a right and just stay on that road. It'll take you into Pawhuska. It's forty-three miles." Sis would finish with a little lift of her chin and give her most charming smile when the traveler reached to shake her hand and offer thanks.

If the lost souls were unfortunate, they'd get Bub, who delighted in getting them even more confused. He knew every back road and ditch within fifty miles of the farm, but for him it was an opportunity to toy with someone's mind. It became an art for my brother and a learning experience for me to listen.

"Oh, Fairfax. Sure, I know where that is. That road up there, just take a left and go about four miles. Or is it five? I don't know, you can't miss it. There's a mail-box on the corner where you turn. Says Johnson. Or Jones. Something with a J. Course, the weeds are kind of grown up around it, but you'll see it. Right there, you make a right, then at the next section, another right, then about three or maybe two miles on you'll come to a pond ..."

Faces, at first gleaming with interest and gratitude, slowly melted into a grimace of something near pain. Some would scramble to their vehicle for paper and pencil, others tried taking mental notes, but they all left with a look of complete astonishment. As they drove away, Bub would wave.

"You betcha, glad to help." When the red dust followed the car out of sight, my brother would start grinning. "Hope they have lots of gasoline. And water."

Once in a great while I would get the joyful opportunity to be first at the gate to see someone, but the gift was always snatched away by either Sis or Bub who, of course, had seniority. But on one celebrated summer night, I was the first one to see and speak with a stranger who became the conversation piece of Osage County for many years to come.

It was August and the heat was unbearable in the house, so when Carolyn decided to spend the night, we made our bed out near the creek. At least outside, we got a small rustle of breeze now and again and the sound of the creek made us feel cooler.

Dad was working hoot-owl shift and when his headlights faded down the gravel road at eleven, Carolyn and I retrieved the romance comic book she'd gotten from one of her cousins. We looked toward the house to make sure Sis had turned off her bedroom light, then we clicked on our flashlight.

Heads together, we giggled our way through the pages, then took out the cheese and crackers we'd snuck from the house.

"My cousin Sharon says you can't kiss boys." Carolyn always had new and interesting information from her Fairfax cousins.

"I don't see the harm in it," I said.

"Have you done it?" Her voice was laced with alarm.

"Well ..."

My friend was shocked. Her eyes widened and she put her hand on her mouth. "Who?"

"Billy V. He kissed me right on the lips down beneath Charley Creek Bridge. It was the swellest kind of feeling."

"Sharon says you can get ... you know."

"Oh," I said, completely daft of her meaning. "What?" I finally asked, stuffing my face with crackers.

"You know ... pregnant." She whispered the word, as if the owls above might hear and descend upon us with wrath.

I choked out a puff of dried crackers and Carolyn pounded me on the back. When I could finally breathe, I walked to the creek and drank several handfuls of water. Carolyn followed me, sticking her bare feet into the trickle of warm creek.

"Your cousin's wrong on that one. Bub told me all about such things a long time ago. Kissin doesn't have squat to do with it. I mean you have to ... well."

"What?" Carolyn scooted closer to me.

"You know. Do it."

"Do what?"

"Breed."

Carolyn let out a gasp and shrunk away from me. For several moments she stared, her brown eyes wide in the moonlight. "You mean like the cows and such?"

"Hard to believe, isn't it? When Bud told me, I thought he was so full of it. But little by little I've pieced it all together. Watching Shorty and Shadow and the animals, reading biology." I leaned back, savoring the sense of my accomplishment.

Carolyn drew her knees up under her chin and rested her head on her hands for several minutes, then, as if the revelation were too much to hold, she yawned. "Reckon I'll go to sleep."

For a long time I lay on top of the quilt with the warm summer breeze teasing my toes and Shorty asleep on my shoulder. I thought about Billy V and how swell he'd been and wondered where he was. I drifted into a peaceful sleep and awoke with a jump.

My dog was stiff beside me and a low, warning growl was erupting from deep in his belly. I blinked my eyes to focus and saw the stiff shadow just above me in the moonlight. I was frozen with fear. If not for my dog, I might have stayed like that the entire night, paralyzed, staring at the shadow.

Shorty finally squeezed from my death grip, wiggling free and taking two stiff-legged steps forward. Hair bristled from neck to tail, he gave a louder warning to the stranger.

His courage somehow gave me strength. I sat up with a jerk. "Who are you? What do you want?" The words jumped out much more forceful than they'd felt in my throat.

"This is my yard," the shadow said. "What are you doing here?"

It was a puzzle. Her words temporarily locked up my thinking gears. When my mind snapped back into place I got an eerie feeling that traveled from my toes to the back of my neck.

Was I dreaming? Like Alice, maybe I was on a wonderful journey in a land that made no sense. The idea excited me and I found my voice. "No, this is my yard and you are the stranger."

The shadow slumped then into a heap beside me and started to whimper. "It's so confusing," she said. "I don't know where I am or who I am or ... who are you?"

"I'm Sissy Gal," I said, extending my hand. By then I had convinced myself it was a full-blown dream and I was about to embark on an adventure. I could barely wait to go on, knowing I'd have so much to tell Carolyn the next morning.

"Who is that?" Carolyn's voice was muffled behind me as she drew the covers up around her face.

The stranger threw back her head and let out a screechy, hysterical laugh. "Twins, oh how wonderful."

That interested me, but Carolyn lost interest in a hurry. She jumped and ran. "I'm gettin Sis." She screamed as she disappeared around the corner.

"How'd you get way out here?" I asked, knowing I was not dreaming and that my older sister would come quickly and steal the stranger away from me.

"It was the boiling water," she said. "And that towel that caught fire."

My sister appeared in the next moment, her night-shirt hanging past her knees and hair in curlers. She held Dad's double-barrel shotgun in her hands. Aiming it at the stranger she said, "Get up."

"You sound like Wyatt Earp," I said. "Don't point that at her. She isn't gonna hurt anybody."

Sis cuffed me on the head. "Shut up and let's all just go in the house."

We were all sitting in the living room when Dad came home at seven-thirty the next morning. Sis in curlers and nightshirt, aiming the shotgun at the stranger. Bub and Carolyn and I sitting on the floor listening to every word our guest had to offer while Lil Bub slept on the couch.

"What in hell's name?" Dad said, taking off his hat and scratching his head. "Who are you?" He walked toward the lady sitting in the corner and offered his hand. She shrank away from him and began to hum an Old South tune.

"She showed up in the middle of the night. Sissy and Carolyn were sleeping in the yard and she just walked up." Sis got a perplexed look on her face then turned away from the woman and lowered her voice. "She's ... crazy. A crazy lady."

Dad looked at the scene before him and shifted his weight from one broganed boot to the other. "What next?" he said. "Sis, you and Sissy get in there and fix some breakfast. Bub and I will take this lady down to the nine-mile and use the phone. Figure out something. We'll be back directly."

So, the story slowly evolved over the next few weeks. The crazy lady had escaped from a place over in Norman, Oklahoma where disturbed people went to get well. She'd somehow gotten out of the hospital and into Osage County. Before she wandered onto our place that night, she'd gone to one of our neighbors and moved the furniture around. The Wilson's came home from a trip and didn't know what to make of it. Their furniture, pictures and dishes were all rearranged, but nothing was missing and no one was there.

The Crazy Lady turned to legend and the tale took on energy as it traveled. Since I was the first one to see her, I became a kind of celebrity. The kids at school begged me over and over to tell them the story. They'd gather around me in a big circle and wait until I'd start.

"She came in the night. A stiff shadow, lurking against the moon." It was probably the beginning of my storytelling abilities, because the attention appealed to me and the joy of adding a color here and a word there gave me a wonderful sense of connectedness to my world. "It was the boiling water," I'd say, in a refined voice, "And that towel I caught on fire."

Many times when I'd go into the details of that night, I'd see my friend Carolyn slink away from the huddle and go off by herself. Where I'd found the crazy lady fascinating, the whole experience bothered my friend. I practiced throwing back my head and copying the lady's laugh until I had it perfected.

"Doesn't that give you the willies?" Carolyn asked, with a forlorn look. "Talking about it and telling it over and over. I mean she was crazy. That's scary."

I didn't understand her reasoning. Maybe because I grew up with people scaring me. It was a way of life around our house. Dad was famous for jumping out from behind dark buildings or putting a dead snake where someone would step on it. And stories about Grandpa Jacobs were part of our family heritage. How he loved to put a sheet over his head and terrorize the kids at night.

Maybe too, the experience with the crazy lady didn't bother me because I felt a kind of responsibility toward her. She was my stranger, so to speak, and I grew quite fond of her.

One bright autumn Saturday when the blackjacks, cottonwoods and scrub oak sparkled with golden reds, I made my way across the field to play with Carolyn Ann. The stream was rushing beneath the bridge and the air was brisk with the promise of change. It was a perfect day to be near the creek with my friend.

Studying Oklahoma history in school had me in the mood for a good game of Indians. I'd collected a few feathers from the woods, stuck them into my braids and stripped off my shirt. "Geronimo," I said to Shorty. Kneeling down, I picked a clump of poke-berries and smeared purple juice on my face. "Soma Sina Woochoo."

My dog agreed with an "errf" but hurried along, anxious to play with his friend, Fly Boy.

Just as we reached the edge of the barn, I heard Cookie's voice and looked up. In the driveway, Frank and Cookie were just leaving.

"Sure you don't want to go to town with us?"

"No. Think I'll stay here and look through these matchbooks Uncle Bud sent, then go to the bridge. Maybe Sissy will be there." Carolyn plopped herself on the stairs and began to look through a sack she held in her hand.

Carolyn's brother Steve climbed in the truck then hung his head out of the window. "Don't let the crazy lady get you."

Carolyn cringed. She looked behind her into the empty house and gave a little shudder.

"Steve, hush," Frank said.

But the words and Carolyn's reaction to them made me stop in my tracks and giggle. The opportunity was perfect. I could give my friend a good scare. I knelt down and grabbed my dog, putting my finger to my lips. We watched as the pickup pulled away and disappeared down the road.

"You stay here, Buddy," I told Shorty. He looked at me with a curious stare. He was always allowed to go into White's yard and visit Carolyn's Fly Boy. "Just wait for me. I'll holler at you."

I watched as Carolyn rattled her fingers through the sack in her lap, pulling out matchbooks and placing them next to her on the porch. I knew if I could sneak up over the terraces and come in through the front door, I'd have it made. I motioned for Shorty to stay then took off in a dead run, bounding out and around.

Once in the house, I peeked through the front room and could still see Carolyn on the steps. I snuck through Frank and Cookie's bedroom and into Carolyn's, just making it out of sight behind the door when I heard her walk back into the kitchen.

Sitting at the dining room table, Carolyn continued through her matchbooks. Carefully looking, putting some in a neat row on the table and tossing others aside, she was hard at work when I accidently bumped her bedroom door with my bare foot. The old door moved forward with a squeak.

Carolyn sat straight up in the chair, her back stiffened. I could see her through the crack and knew my opportunity had arrived. I threw back my head and let out an exact replica of the crazy lady's hysterical laugh.

My friend jumped up so quickly her chair went banging backward on the hardwood floor. She let out a little scream and bolted toward the door. Looking back as she ran, she hit the heavy oak coffee table with both knees and let out a painful squall. She began to crawl as fast as she could, hitting the screen door with her head and going out across the porch and into the yard on hands and knees.

It was all I could do running to catch up with Carolyn's crawl. I tried yelling her name, but the sound of something behind her sent her spiraling to her feet and off across the field like a rabbit. Finally, I stopped laughing and put my heart into the run and tackled her near the school yard in the fresh-plowed wheat field.

I was breathing so hard I could barely speak. "It ... was just a joke," I said, rubbing sweaty pokeberry juice from my face and pulling feathers from my hair.

She turned to me and her wide, brown eyes narrowed into slits. "Go Home!"

"But, Carolyn, I ... it was just a joke. I didn't mean for you to hurt yourself. It was all in fun. I thought we could play Geronimo ..."

My best friend stood and gathered a handful of dirt clods. Drawing back, she pelted me around the feet and legs. "Go Home," she said.

In the months I'd known Carolyn, she'd never thrown one clod. She refused to fight with anyone. By nature she was bashful and quiet. Her reaction sent me retreating in confusion.

Carolyn's anger frustrated me. I felt sure she would be fine the next day, but she wasn't. And two weeks

later she still refused to talk to me. At school, she
played with Grace Ann, Lucy May, or Linda Kay and
she'd ignore me anytime I'd try to join in.

One afternoon I went down to the bridge alone. It
seemed strange being there without Carolyn. We'd discovered the place together, made it our meeting spot,
and filled it with our most treasured possessions. I took
my finger and traced the chalk drawings Carolyn and I
had made on the bridge wall. The maps led to our hide-
outs along the river. Places where we'd become blood
brothers, taken secret oaths, and exchanged vows to always be friends.

I sat on our bedsprings pulling Shorty into my lap.
"Let's play house, Buddy." I said, jumping up with enthusiasm. I jerked pots and cracked dishes from beneath the washing machine frame and began to gather
mud for pies. But Shorty took off after a scurrying field
mouse and left me with my thoughts.

Memories drifted over me as I looked from the bedsprings to the washing machine frame to the cracked
dishes. Carolyn and I had discovered our furnishings in
an old dump along the Arkansas River. It took days of
work to drag the things all the way up the creek to our
bridge.

In the spring the rising waters from rain storms
would pick our treasures up, carry them back toward
the river, and deposit them in mysterious places along
our creek banks. It was great fun for Carolyn and me to
set out in search of our bedsprings, washing machine
frame and various pans and dishes then return them to

our bridge every year. Thoughts of us giggling down the creek and squealing with joy made my sore heart ache.

Bub appeared just as I splashed water on my face to wash away the tears. "What's up, Sissy Gal?"

"The bridge isn't much fun now, Bub."

"Carolyn still mad at you?" He kind of grinned.

"It isn't funny, Bub. I miss her somethan terrible. She's hurt my feelins and it's the worst kind of sad in the world." The words jarred loose more emotions.

My brother knelt for a minute letting me snot and sniff and wash my face again with creek water.

"Have you thought about how you hurt her feelins? That day you scared her?"

I looked at him. "I did?"

"You know how Dad scares you sometimes with snakes? How you detest them? Doesn't that make you mad enough to want to bite a nail in two?"

A surge of anger rose up at the most recent memory of Dad putting a dead snake on the step, then hollering for me to come outside. "That does make me mad. Real mad. It isn't funny, Bub."

"No."

"Why do you suppose he does it? He seems to think it's funny," I said.

Bub hesitated, pulling a Snicker from his overalls pocket. He broke the candy bar in half, offering me a delightful chunk of the chewy chocolate caramel. "I reckon because his Daddy did it to him and thought it was funny. It's what he learned, so he thinks its OK."

"But if his daddy did it and taught him and our daddy does it to us, then how was I suppose to know not to do it to Carolyn?"

Bub let out a loud laugh that echoed off the cool bridge walls and bounced down the creek into the trees.

"I should know by now not to get in these conversations with you, Sissy. No matter what, you can always complicate things to a point of confusion." He started walking off, wallowing the candy around in his mouth, shaking his head.

"What should I do, Bub? About Carolyn? I want to fix things."

"If it were me, I reckon I'd say, 'Sorry'."

"What if she doesn't listen?"

"I'd keep on sayin it as many times as it takes for her to believe me."

Then my brother left me alone sitting with my feet in the creek enjoying the sweet candy. His words fired me with determination. I jumped and set a brisk stride toward the White farm. Walking up across the terraces with Shorty by my side, I heard Fly Boy barking a welcome as we crested the hill.

Carolyn happened to be in the yard. When she saw me, she turned abruptly and started for the house, then she did an about face and marched across the field right toward me. My heart quickened with anticipation, hoping she was coming to play.

When she got within twenty feet of me, she reached down and grabbed a handful of clods. Pelting me first around the feet, she screamed, "Go Home. You aren't my friend anymore."

"Sorry I scared you." I screamed back, walking right into the barrage of fire. "Sorry, I scared you. Sorry, I scared you." The clods kept coming, harder and faster, rising upward to my belly, my shoulders, my face. I kept walking toward her. "Sorry, Sorry, Sorry." I screamed.

When neither of us gave ground, we finally were face-to-face. Tears burst from my dirt-splotched eyes. "Dad scares us with snakes and such and that's because his dad scared him and I thought it was okay. I didn't know." The brown eyes in front of me still sparked with anger. We stared.

Shorty and Fly Boy came streaking past us, ripping up across the terraces, romping with play. They cut circles around and around us then took off in the direction of the bridge, barking out an invitation.

"OK." Carolyn finally said, taking a step backward, dropping a clod and brushing the dirt from her hands.

Wiping dust from my face with the sleeve of my shirt, I looked at her, not knowing what to expect.

"OK," she repeated. She walked several steps across the field in the direction of the bridge then stopped and turned. "You comin?"

They were the best two words I'd ever heard.

The crazy lady's visit had a huge impact on my life. She taught me the value of friendship, how fragile it can be, and how sometimes something we've learned has to be unlearned. I found that apologizing, speaking those two small words, is a lot of work. But once said, the apology can sweep away every trace of hurt feelings, like wisping dust with a feather duster.

Because of the stranger in the night, I had my first experience with storytelling and I began to think about a lot of old things in new ways. It seemed to me that the crazy lady was interesting and quite sane in some ways, while some of the rest of us could be rigid and a little bit crazy.

V

After the crazy lady's visit, Dad had a phone put in at the farm. The shining black oddity hung on the kitchen wall just inside the doorway.

"This is the number you call at work." Dad taped a small piece of notebook paper next to the phone. "In case some stranger rambles in again at night or one of you kids need a doctor, you can call. Those are the only two reasons you bother me at work."

His words hung in the silence for a few minutes as the four of us sat around the kitchen table, digesting the rules. Then, he looked right at Bub and Sis, "It's not a plaything. We're on a party line so I better not hear from one of our neighbors that you two were on here jabbering with friends. And if you pick the receiver up and someone is talking, gently put it back down. Mind your manners."

Sis and Bub nodded in agreement with looks of earnest obedience. The second Dad left for work that afternoon, all hell broke loose. Sis and Bub stood by the

screen door and waited until Dad's truck faded from
sight, then they both dived toward the kitchen, scuffling and hanging onto each other, trying to be first on
the phone.

I couldn't for the life of me understand the attraction. Carolyn told me to call her the next morning before I walked to the bridge. I wasted the best part of an
hour lifting up the phone then gently putting it down
because it was busy. The waiting made me impatient
and irritated. Finally, when I did call, Carolyn's line was
busy. Then Sis and Bub were fighting over the phone
again. It was afternoon when Shorty and I finally burst
out of the house and stomped off across the terraces to
my friend's house.

"Don't ask me to call anymore. I don't like that stupid phone. What's the fun of it? I could have walked
over here and we'd been at the bridge hours ago."

But my fourteen-year-old brother and sixteen-
year-old sister worshiped the new piece of black plastic
on the wall. Sis would go through this great ritual of
setting all her nail polish and remover, lipstick, and various tools in a neat little row on the table, making herself a glass of iced tea, then calling one of a dozen
friends to talk about boys.

Bub's calls were to one of two neighbor girls. He
would take the phone off the hook and stretch the cord
to the bathroom until it was as tight and straight as
barbed wire on a new fence. With great effort, he could
maneuver the phone through the crack at the bottom of
the door, slam and lock the bathroom door, and talk for
hours to Lois Marie or Priscilla.

Sis often would come in and press down the button on the phone, disconnecting Bub, who would then fly out of the bathroom and attack Sis. My brother, on the other hand, enjoyed walking in, catching Sis with her array of cosmetics on the table, and clicking the phone off then running out the door, which sent my sister into a state of hysteria.

Sometimes both of them would share the receiver, as they listened and listened to the neighbors' conversations, snickering behind their hands.

"Oh these dreadful hot flashes," Bub would mock in a feminine voice after eavesdropping. "Men don't have to worry with such things. They don't know how lucky they are."

"Well, dear," Sis would take up the other end of the conversation. "When you've got a straight gut and a strong back, what's there to worry about?"

Then the two of them would crumble with howls of laughter.

Before the arrival of the phone that summer, my sister had first grabs on our horse, Maybelle. She was the oldest and it did little good to argue. Carolyn and I always yearned to include Maybelle in our many pretend games, so with the distraction of the phone, we were able to sneak off with the horse more often without repercussions from Sis.

When my sister made up her mind to ride over and meet Arlene or Ora Lee, she would find us, snatch Maybelle without even asking, and ride away, brushing off our screaming protests with a wave of her hand.

My older brother, who had never cared that much for Maybelle, began to enter the competition for the horse about that same time. His phone calls to Lois Marie and Priscilla had apparently put him in need of better transportation. But he not only wanted the horse, he wanted a driver. Insecure with his horsemanship abilities, he would talk me into managing the reins while he rode on back.

So poor Maybelle usually became our prisoner in the wee morning hours. She found herself bridled most of the day, shifted from pillar to post, shuffled from one of us to the other, and often caught in the middle of lengthy, heated confrontations.

God certainly knew what he was doing when he sent that particular horse to us four as a gift through my aunt Eunice in Arkansas. Registered as a quarter horse, Maybelle was a golden palomino with white mane and tale. But her beauty went way beyond her splendid appearance. A more patient, forgiving animal has never walked the face of this earth.

Without a saddle, the four of us had to invent ways to jump aboard the big horse. Sis and Bub usually led the mare next to a fence or a stump or into a gully. Maybelle would cooperate completely, moving her big body as close as possible to make it easy.

Around the age of five, I began to experiment with better ways to mount Maybelle. Sometimes I would dive off of the horse's back in the middle of the field to examine a wildflower or pick up a dead butterfly. On those occasions, I'd have to walk all the way back to the fence or into the trees to remount.

After much practice, I discovered that if I bounced high enough with little short jumps, I could just manage to grab the ends of Maybelle's long white mane.

Clinging like a turtle to a tadpole, I'd start up her knees with my bare toes and scramble my way up. She would often assist by dropping her head and then lifting it with a kind of elevator effect as I emerged toward the top.

Carolyn and I also liked to lead Maybelle under a tree limb, climb the tree, then plop down on her back. The big golden horse was always obliging. If she ever moved at all it would be toward you to make the effort easier.

Maybelle's arrival on the farm came in 1950 when I was two and Lil Bub wasn't born yet. She came to us in the back of a pickup equipped only with flimsy stock racks. A weanling, never away from the protection of her mother, the wild-eyed filly backed out of the truck dancing nervously. While Dad and Mama held and petted her to quiet her fears, I apparently toddled up between her back legs, sat on the ground with one small arm around each leg and declared, "I love you Mamey Mell."

The young horse could have torn me to pieces if she had moved. Instead, Maybelle turned around, looked at me, and Mama swears she gave out a contented sigh. She must have known she was home.

Dad's favorite story about our horse concerned Mama and an old saddle that had once hung on the corral fence near the barn. Baked for an unknown number of years beneath the summer sun, then rained on all winter, Dad described the piece of leather as an ancient lizard.

Mama, who always had a playful, inventive mind, got the idea one day to make a cinch for the saddle using baling twines braided together. When she finished her invention, she decided to try it out by saddling Maybelle and riding her up through the wheat field to take Dad a Mason jar of iced tea.

Dad could never tell the story without laughing. "Here comes your mother, trotting along with her jar of tea jangling, grinning from ear to ear. 'Ride em cowboy,' she calls out when she sees me looking. About that time the cinch slipped and the saddle fell beneath Maybelle's belly. Your Mama was hanging upside down, tea dripping from her face. With both feet hung in the old stirrups and her back on the ground, she was trapped. Maybelle turned and looked, curious, then began to munch grass."

In the summer of 1958, on a muggy August afternoon, Maybelle proved that even she had a limit.

Carolyn and I had snuck away with the horse early that morning, determined to include Maybelle in a game of Indians we had planned. Just in the middle of our staged battle, with the cowboy (Lil Bub) riding innocently under the cottonwood trees near our granary, Carolyn and I (Cochise and Geronimo) had just emerged squalling from the trees and pounced on Maybelle's back behind Lil Bub, hacking at him with our spears and assorted homemade weapons.

Sis appeared, jerking Maybelle out from under our tree and disrupting our entire scene. "Get off! I'm meeting Arlene in Hadden's pasture and I'm late."

I looked down at my sister and let out an Indian squall. Kicking Maybelle in the flank, I held onto my little brother and Carolyn grabbed me around the waist from behind. Although Maybelle never was one to get in a big hurry, the kick must have startled her, because she took off at a fast trot.

Hiding in the blackjack thicket, we all watched in silence for a few moments until we saw my sister's speck appear on the horizon.

"She's hoppin mad," Lil Bub said.

"I don't care. I'm sick of her buttin into our games anytime she wants. Let her chase us for awhile. Maybe she'll get discouraged and leave us be."

"Got ya," Bub's voice growled out of the nearby ditch. He jumped right up in Maybelle's face, grabbing the bridle reins. "You guys have had your turn, now get off. Sissy, I want you to ride me over to Lois Marie's."

"No," I said, defiantly. "We're in the middle of our game and we aren't gonna get off. Besides, I'm tired of taking you over to see your girlfriends."

My brother grabbed my leg and pulled, which caused the three of us to start sliding. I kicked Maybelle and she sidestepped, dragging Bub along with us. By wiggling, slapping and kicking, I finally managed to detach Bub from Maybelle and we were off once again.

We didn't get far. The distraction allowed Sis to spot us and she closed in before we could hit the open field. In the next few minutes, a battle of wills shattered the summer stillness.

Sis on one side jerked on a rein and Bub yanked on Maybelle's other rein, while Lil Bub hung on Maybelle's neck and I kicked and screamed, Carolyn clinging to my back. Maybelle jumped in wide circles, trying to miss two sets of bare feet while she worried with three little bodies bouncing around up above.

For weeks, our horse had endured endless hours of relentless work. If not tied to the front fence in the smoldering heat, she was on her way to Hadden's pasture or the Wilson's or Speakman's miles away or patiently bouncing along while wild Indians whacked and screamed above her. She had to graze at night and steal a nap between our escapades.

Something long overdue snapped in Maybelle that afternoon. In the midst of our battle, she stopped dead still. With a little jump she dislodged Sis and Bub from the reins, then she took off in a gentle trot toward a low branch of a cottonwood tree near the creek. She slowed, walked beneath the branch and gently scraped the three of us off her back. Then turning, to make sure her cargo was safely deposited in the soft mud, she bounded off in a dead run, kicking and twisting like a rodeo bucking bronc.

Sis and Bub tried catching her for hours that afternoon while Carolyn and Lil Bub and I watched from our tree house. Maybelle would let them get about three feet from her then run like Dad's rooster after his dip in the horse tank. After while they both gave up and called it a day.

The next morning, Dad woke us all early and made the announcement as he flipped corn cakes at the stove. "I have a surprise for you kids."

We seldom saw Dad excited or happy during those days after Mama left, so his enthusiasm and grin made us all stop and stare.

"The 101 Ranch Rodeo Parade is being held this afternoon in Ponca City. We're all gonna go. Dick, one of my friends from the railroad, is coming out with his horse trailer. He and I are going to walk in the parade as trappers, leading his bloodhounds. Bub, you and Lil Bub can walk with us. You girls have always wanted to ride Maybelle in a parade. This is your chance."

Sis let out a little squeal of pleasure and bounded up from the table. "I have to iron a shirt and pick out some jeans. Come on, Sissy, let's see what you can wear."

I jumped and ran, my heart pounding with pure joy. Ponca City. The parade. Crowds of happy people lined up for miles to see the floats and bands and silver-saddled horses ... and I would be part of it.

The morning turned into a flurry of activity. The boys came in and out of the house, rummaging through their bedrooms for coonskin caps and pellet guns while Sis fussed over her old clothes and changed her mind three times about which shirt she'd wear.

When Dad's friend, Dick, drove up the driveway with a two-horse trailer, my father had just begun whistling for Maybelle. Our good-natured horse, who would usually come trotting at the first sound of a beckoning whistle, didn't even look up from where she grazed beneath the pecan trees.

"We're ready, Dick." Dad grinned. "Here, Sissy, go fetch Maybelle."

I took the halter, casting a wary glance at Sis who came out of the house behind me. "Come on," Sis said, "I'll help you. This is gonna be SO much fun."

But Maybelle hadn't forgiven us yet. When we approached she didn't even look up. Instead she continued grazing until we got about three feet away then she took off in a dead run, romping and kicking.

Before Sis and I could discuss the situation, Dad and Dick and my brothers were joining us. "What in hell's name has gotten into her?" Dad bellowed, looking straight at Sis. He had an intuitive response to such things. "She's never run like that in her entire life. What have you kids done to her?"

I gave my half-smile, raised-eyebrow look of innocence and all of us remained quiet.

"We've still got a little time." Dick volunteered. "Let's just all drive her toward the corral and catch her there."

It sounded like a simple enough plan. The six of us spread out and closed in around the golden mare, easing our way up behind her softly. Again, Maybelle waited patiently until we were within a few short feet, then she snorted, ripped and took off running, but instead of heading in the direction of the barn, bolted back to the south right past Lil Bub who was waving his arms and yelling.

"That beats any damn thing I've ever seen," Dad said, and his earlier good disposition was taking on a tinge of darkness. "I swear, Dick, she's the gentlest horse in the county. I don't know what's gotten into her." He looked at us again. It was a lingering look full of quiet accusation and it made my feet itch.

"Sissy, run to the barn and fetch a half bucket of that sweet feed in the barrel by the loft."

I took off as fast as my feet could run, stopping only after I reached the barn, and struggled to fill a bucket. Maybelle had to go to the parade. It might be our one and only chance.

Dad handed the bucket to Sis. "Here, you're the one who rides her most. Catch your horse."

Sis had a look of quiet desperation. She'd tried the feed bucket trick the day before and it didn't work. I held my breath as she approached Maybelle, talking gently in a pleading voice. When she had the halter fastened tightly around Maybelle's neck, I exhaled.

Dad's mood seemed to lighten again and he laughed and talked to Dick as Sis led Maybelle toward the trailer. On the few occasions our mare had been loaded into a horse trailer, it was a simple task. Dad would drape the lead rope up over her neck, slap her on the butt and she'd crawl right in without a moment's hesitation.

When Dad slapped Maybelle on the rump and told her to load, she stood like a stone. "Get on in there," Dad said, raising his voice and thumping the horse harder. Maybelle acted like she'd been poured and set in cement. She didn't try to run, didn't dance around. She simply didn't move.

Dad gave a nervous laugh and looked at Dick. "You probably don't believe this, but she's always loaded without a minute's trouble."

My Irish-German father was trying very hard to keep his temper, something he wasn't that accomplished at doing. He slapped Maybelle more gently, two or three little love pats on the rump, "Get on in there, girl. We're going to the parade."

Maybelle didn't respond. My father didn't lose it all at once, it was a gradual unthreading over the next thirty minutes that ended with him bellowing and whacking our horse on the back legs with a green switch. Finally, as if Maybelle calmly decided in her own time to allow my Dad to win, she stepped nonchalantly up in the horse trailer.

Dad's face was red and dripping with sweat, his shirt had large wet stains under both arms and down the back and all of his earlier, festive attitude had disappeared when we all crowded into Dick's pickup and started to Ponca City.

Everyone was laughing and talking as Dick weaved his way in and out of the side streets trying to find the end of the great mass of humanity lining up for the parade. It was the most people I'd ever seen in one place.

"The horses are in the front," a policeman directed from the street corner when Dick rolled down his window and asked. "I think you trappers will be just behind the horses. You'll have to park your outfit around First Street. The parade will cross the railroad tracks and go all the way down Grand to Fourteenth."

After some expert maneuvering, the pickup was parked and we unloaded Maybelle. Dick and Dad, in old overalls and brogan boots, wore sweat-stained hats. Dick untied his bloodhounds from the back of the truck, gave one leash to Dad, then each of them slung a moonshine jug over one shoulder.

"Look, everyone but us has a saddle," Sis said, loud enough for Dad to hear. She'd been begging for a saddle for as long as I could recall. It was another opportunity to get the idea across.

"Just be glad you've got a horse," Dad said, helping Lil Bub with his coonskin cap.

As I looked at the huge clump of horses gathering, I thought to myself, "*Who cares about an old saddle. We've got the prettiest pony in the bunch.*" Sis and I brushed Maybelle's long white mane until it shined like silk. We rubbed on her golden coat with a rag until she gleamed in the bright afternoon sun.

When the parade started, Sis and I sat on Maybelle and watched. My eyes darted like dragonflies. First to the floats congregating on either side of us then to the many sparkling silver saddles and fancy-dressed cowboys. I could barely breathe my heart was pounding so fast and I squirmed around behind Sis so much, turning my head this way and that, she finally swatted me on the leg. "You're like a worm in hot ashes. Sit still."

Then we were walking. Sis let Maybelle fall right in behind a sequined lady riding a big gray gelding. I chanced one look back, but couldn't see Dad and my brothers because they were way behind the long line of horses.

Things went swimmingly for one block. When we reached the railroad tracks, Maybelle stopped. She looked down at the gleaming strips of iron sparkling in the sun and took two slow steps backward. Sis nudged her gently with the heel of her boot and patted her shoulder. "It's OK, girl. It's just a railroad. It won't hurt you."

"Come on girl," I pleaded, nudging Maybelle gently in the flank with my heel.

But our friend Maybelle had no intention of crossing the ominous steel line that stretched before her into eternity. She looked at it first one way then the other, her eyes so wide the white showed, then I felt her go rigid beneath my thighs. She'd had a rough week and this was the end of her patience.

"Get her on up there," the rider behind us hollered. "You're holding up the line."

Two men riding identical black horses with studded saddles appeared out of nowhere. One grabbed Maybelle's bridle and the other got behind and slapped her rump with his quirt, but Maybelle stood, once again frozen into her concrete frame of mind.

Dad and Dick appeared. Word had gotten back to them that a big palomino mare wouldn't cross the railroad track. My father was always a take-charge kind of guy. He didn't hesitate. Doubling the reins in his hand, he grabbed Maybelle near the bridle bit and yanked. "Get on over there."

Maybelle took one quick step and came down on my dad's foot. Dad let out a series of squalls that echoed above the marching band behind us, giving a distorted effect to the nearby audience.

"Oh, you son-of-a ..." Dad was hammering on Maybelle's shoulder, but she stood solid, mashing the toes of Dad's left foot into the pavement. The parade marshal gave a hand signal from his horse and the streaming procession split and started around us. From my vantage point I watched baton twirling girls, gleaming trombones and heard the rhythmic pounding of drums as a steady line of mixed activity trailed by laughing and pointing at us.

Dick and Bub and Dad continued to hammer on poor Maybelle who now seemed paralyzed with fear. Two other large men in uniforms stopped. Both of them were well over six feet, muscular and solid with burr haircuts. They put their shoulders on Maybelle and tried to push her, but she wouldn't budge an inch.

Dad's loud cursing and ranting dwindled slowly into a whispered prayer. "Please," he asked, looking plaintively into Maybelle's wide eyes. "You're killing me."

Finally, four men on horseback rode up. "You girls get off," one man said, trying to mask a look of amusement. He took a lariat, skillfully draped it in a loop over Maybelle's rump, dallied it around his saddle horn and told his horse to "Back up."

Within seconds, Maybelle's rear went to one side, she stepped to keep her balance and poor Dad landed on the railroad track, pale, shaken, but free.

It was a quiet ride back to the farm that afternoon except for Lil Bub who whimpered in disappointment from Sis's lap.

Dad hobbled back to unload Maybelle and when she backed out of the trailer he gave her a despicable look. "You been eating locoweed or something?"

"She's still mad," Lil Bub said, "Because of yesterday."

I felt Sis stiffen beside me and Bub drew in a little gasp of wind.

Dad's face took on a kind of purple hue as he looked from Dick to Lil Bub to us. He let out a ragged sigh and shook his friend's hand. "Well, Dick, thanks for the effort. Sorry about everything."

Dick gave an understanding nod. "Don't worry about it. There'll be other parades."

As the red dust from Dick's pickup faded from sight, I was trying to shush Lil Bub with a squinted stare. The technique fell short. He began to babble like a goose.

"It was all because of yesterday. Sis and Bub yanking Maybelle around while me and Carolyn and Sissy were trying to ride her. Then they chased her most all of the afternoon. It's the phone that started it all." My four-year-old brother's voice took on a passionate urgency. He had lots of valuable information and was in a hurry to share it with Dad.

"What about the phone, Lil Bub?" Dad asked.

"They've been fightin over it from the first. Always on it talkin to someone or listenin to the neighbors ..." He went on and on, each word striking fear in the hearts of at least two of his listeners.

"That's good you told me Lil Bub," Dad said, in a tempered tone. "Now you and Sissy run along. Sissy, you take Maybelle and give her some grain before you turn her loose. Sounds like she deserves a little ... vacation from all of you."

I never knew exactly what Dad said to my older brother and sister that day, but I could imagine. What I do know is, neither of them touched the phone for weeks after that, they left my little brother and me alone, both had extra chores, and they couldn't ride the horse.

Lil Bub and Carolyn and I decided Maybelle needed a paid vacation. We snuck her a little feed every day, gave her long, cool baths from the water hose and I told her stories about fanciful unicorns who flew over scary railroad tracks.

VI

Around the age of ten, I received an invitation from one of the girls at school to go to a revival. Dee was a chubby girl, one year my senior, who had moved to Osage County a few months before. I'd been to her house on a couple of occasions. She was easy enough to be around and had a nice family, so when she asked me to go to church with her, I agreed.

My previous experiences with church had been pleasant. When Mama was home she'd introduced us to a brief sample of Vacation Bible School at a church in Ponca City. We talked of Jesus, colored and cut out pictures, and had wonderful sugar cookies and lemonade.

Starting at age five, I was allowed to ride the passenger train on the Santa Fe Railroad about one hundred fifty miles south to Purcell and visit Grandma Carrie. Since Dad worked on the railroad as a switchman, he knew the conductors and most of the employees along the way. He would take me to the railroad station where he introduced me to all his fellow workers. In my best dress and shining pair of shoes, I'd smile and dip my head.

"This is my youngest girl. Sissy this is ..."

He'd take me on the train himself, seat me and wink at the conductor. "Might find this gal a soda pop along the way." He'd hand the dark-skinned man a quarter.

The large Negro conductors with their light palms and black eyes always showed bright rows of shining teeth, smiling as they took tickets. My fellow travelers whispered behind maps and rummaged through baggage.

After the train was well on its way south, my ears tuned in for the jingle of the cart. The small man who came down the aisle pushing his glorious wagon of icy soda pop, candy bars, cookies, and sandwiches wasn't on any particular schedule, but I knew he'd show up sooner or later.

I devoured every detail of every moment, soaking in the sights and sounds so I could later sit beneath my willow tree near the creek and entertain Lil Bub and Carolyn with my worldly travels.

Grandma Carrie, who never learned to drive, would walk the mile to the train station and meet me. Always wearing a dress, my dad's mother wore her long hair braided on the back of her neck in a bun. In her seventies, she walked like a young woman, holding her head proudly, shoulders still straight.

The light of love would radiate from the first moment our eyes met. I had no doubt where I stood with Grandma Carrie.

"Reckon we better stop at the grocery store so we're sure to have something to eat this week," she'd say.

I agreed with an eager nod, knowing what that meant. She'd let me pick and choose from a wide variety of "store bought" goodies from sweet rolls to ice cream bars.

Everyone along the way would greet her with great respect.

"Good morning, Mrs. Jacobs. How are you today?"

"Fine thank you. This is my little granddaughter came on the train all the way from Osage County near Ponca City."

People would lean down and shake my hand, fussing over my naturally curly hair and blue eyes. I'd stand taller and grin. Being the center of attention was a new feeling for me and one I quickly adjusted to.

Everything at Grandma's seemed sweet. Her cozy home on Adams Street nestled in rose bushes; iris and a blush of perennials beckoned to me like a gingerbread house. Inside, the smell of lemon drops and lilacs lingered as the curtains in the kitchen ruffled in the breeze. My life on the farm seemed slightly disordered, but at Grandma Carrie's the days were as smooth as her polished silver.

Church was the center of my grandmother's existence. She went to the Church of Christ every Sunday morning and evening and on Wednesday evenings. The sermons were boring and I often found myself daydreaming or nodding off into a peaceful snooze. But I loved walking hand in hand to church with Grandma and basking in the attention of all her friends as she bragged on me. It wrapped me in a feeling of warmth and sweet security that I never experienced at home.

Grandma kept her fat Bible next to her recliner, and although she didn't preach to anyone, she often sat and read the pages with a look of complete peace and serenity.

One summer she told me she'd pay me a silver dollar if I memorized the books of the New Testament. I did it within three days and when the preacher came by for a visit she had me recite my accomplishment and glowed with satisfaction.

Later that same day I asked her why reading the Bible made her feel so good.

"It gives me hope about heaven and a sense of why we're here."

"I don't understand most of it," I admitted.

She gave out a great giggle and took me on her lap. "It doesn't matter," she said. "You keep turning to it through the years, someday it will begin to make sense."

After that, I felt more comfortable with all the mystery surrounding God and the Bible. In church, I was under no pressure to know and understand everything. It was a process and I was just beginning.

So when the neighbor girl, Dee, and her mother picked me up that night, I wasn't the least bit afraid to walk into a new church with total strangers. I had only one stipulation.

"My dog Shorty goes with me everywhere," I said to Dee's mother. "Is it OK if he comes to church?"

"He goes to school with her," Dee told her mother. "Sits by her desk everyday."

The lady chuckled and shrugged. "I've never seen a dog in church, but I don't know of a rule against it. Maybe Shorty will find the Lord tonight."

Her words made me slightly uncomfortable that evening when I crawled into the backseat of their car. I'd never heard anyone talk about God in that way. Like you could find Him somewhere out in the woods.

But getting to go anywhere was a rare treat for me, so I settled myself in the car with high expectations. Sis had helped me get dressed and braided my hair into one fat twist down my back. I didn't often wear a dress, but the occasion seemed to call for it, so I chose one Grandma made for me. The fabric was white and adorned with small purple flowers. The dress had puffy elbow length sleeves and a nice lace collar that made me feel pretty.

I had even bathed and brushed my dog, dressing him in his leather collar and leash. Shorty loved people and was always open for rides in the car, so he smiled up at me, sparkling clean in my lap.

Before we even got up the narrow gravel road and pulled out on the highway, Dee's mother asked the question.

"Have you ever been saved, Sissy?"

It seemed like an odd question to me for someone to just ask out of the blue. But I tried answering it the best I could.

"Well, I reckon so." I said, thinking of the time Dad pulled me from the pond. I was five and jumped from the diving board and couldn't swim.

"That's wonderful," she said. "Isn't that wonderful, Dee?"

"I've been considering it," Dee said.

That was perplexing to me. How could someone "consider" getting saved? Did you first think of a way to get yourself in trouble? Bub would certainly be a hand at that, I decided. He had a knack for trouble.

At the church house, light steamed into the cool winter night and a hum of friendly people welcomed us as we took a seat.

"This is our little neighbor friend, Sissy," Dee's mom said and with a nervous laugh added, "She brought her dog, Shorty. We thought Shorty might get saved tonight."

As we seated ourselves and the talking simmered to whispers and slowly died to silence, her words kept tripping through my mind. What had she said earlier? About Shorty finding the Lord. Now she was talking about the saved thing. *"Interesting,"* I thought. *"It must be something to do with their religion."* With my limited experience it didn't occur to me that churches could have drastic differences.

In my crisp dress, with freshly washed hair and my dog near me, I felt a great sense of well-being. Pleasant memories of Grandma lingered in my mind as the preacher stepped to the pulpit. He was a great tall man with bushy eyebrows and hair. His clothes hung on his thin frame like a coat on a hat rack and he had a drawn, serious expression that caused me to stare.

"Praise God," he screamed and his huge baritone voice rattled to the rafters. A murmur of voices echoed the words all around and I turned quickly, shocked that people would talk during church. After a few minutes, things got quiet.

The giant preacher stood scowling. His eyes sifted over the congregation, and when he saw me, the piercing blue sparks lingered. "Everyone here tonight has the opportunity to meet Jezzzuss." He sung out the last word and it brought a rattling rip from the audience. Some screamed, "Amen" and "Praise God," while others stood and started saying strange things that I couldn't understand.

I pulled my dog up closer to me and took a death grip on his collar.

"Some of you, out of the pure meanness of your sinning hearts, will go to HELLLL. Will BURN in HELLLL before you walk this aisle."

His word made a tingling chill inch its way up my back like a caterpillar crawling on a branch. My mouth went dry and Shorty, who'd settled himself in for a nice nap, sat up and began to look around, curious about the commotion.

After a few more death-like silences followed by outbursts from the preacher and rattling echoes from the congregation, I relaxed just a little. It was a strange church, but not at all boring. If I observed close enough, I could later reenact the scene and greatly entertain my brothers and sister.

So I begin to make note of the many words that blasted out of his mouth, the syntax and emphasis. I watched people around me jump in response, raise their hands wildly, and babble in a half-Apache-half-Dutch language. Shorty seemed just as intrigued and injected a little "errf" here and a "yelp" there.

Just as I was back to thoroughly enjoying myself, a lady in the front row let out a wail, walked to the center of the aisle below the preacher's pulpit, and fell in a heap. That sent the entire church into an eruption of screams and squalls of every variety. They were coming so fast I couldn't make note of them all in my mind.

The next thing that happened was truly amazing. A young man got right down in the aisle and rolled over and over on the floor. Shorty and I watched with amazement and my dog began barking, caught up in the emotional high that was ricocheting from the ceiling to the floor. Another lady walked to the aisle and flopped around on the floor like a fish out of water. More and more people filed down the row toward the preacher and each time the people would erupt into howls of glory and amens.

A great spirit rose up in me like the feeling I sometimes got when I stripped my shirt, painted my face with pokeberries, and made up Indian songs. I stood, lifted my head, and let out a howl. "Hey Yauche Kye Monta Shay."

Immediately, Dee stood and latched onto my hand. "Isn't it wonderful, Sissy Gal?" She had great tears running down her face and she let out a little sob. "Won't you come?"

She began to drag me toward the center aisle where her Mother had already disappeared. Dee outweighed me by fifty pounds and she was built square as a post. Once she got a grip on my hand it was impossible for me to dislodge her, so away we went, her weeping and pulling and me sliding like a colt new to a lead rope.

Getting caught up in the spirit was one thing. Trailing down and facing the bushy-browed angry preacher was another. I'd never been one to like standing at the front of the room with everyone watching.

My efforts were futile, though. Dee continued to bull her way down the aisle through the crowd, dragging me, my feet leaving skid marks on the waxed hardwood floor. I had a death grip on Shorty's leash and he was bringing up the rear, feet also planted and a look of terror on his face.

At the front of the church there was a line of weepers, howlers, and rollers. Each moved along until they reached the giant who would bend over them. The person would say something to the preacher, then drop to their knees. The giant would put a skillet hand on top of the person's head, look up, and babble something that brought new shrieks and screams from the audience.

As the line dwindled and Dee pulled me closer and closer to the front, I tried to bolt. Once I jerked away and might have escaped but for a wide-hipped lady behind who stood like an iron wall. I bumped her once, twice, the adrenalin coursing through my veins and the thought of flight just within reach, then Dee had me again, secure in her iron grasp.

My poor dog began to bark in despair. He was getting jerked first this way then that, throttled along in the traffic with people stepping on him and pushing him out of the way.

Then we were at the front of the line. The preacher was towering over me, bending down. I looked up, not knowing what to say. He stood and frowned until his eyebrows formed a solid line of dark brush. His eyes were owlish, peering down from the darkness of a great tree. "What do you have to say?"

Panic rose up in me and I reeled my dog in by the leash, jerking him up in my arms and squeezing him until he groaned. The giant had me by the shoulder, his huge fingers biting into my skin.

"Young lady, what do you have to say?" He screamed above the roaring crowd.

"Awoomey Bawla Caw. Soma Sina Woo Choo." I wailed.

The big preacher got a forlorn look of bewilderment on his face. For one horrible moment the entire church quieted. My knees quaked beneath me and I thought I'd puke. Then Dee, who stood at my right side still connected to my hand, whispered, "Amen."

In the next instant the whole church descended upon me shaking my hand, shrieking, and bawling. Shorty was trembling and whining to get some relief.

"My dog needs to ... be excused." I said. Dee turned loose of my hand; Shorty and I made our exit. Standing out in the night air with the cool wind against my sweaty face, I took a deep breath and felt relief wash through me. Shorty whined and walked a few steps toward the car, wagging his tail. We were both ready to go.

On the ride home Dee and her mother went on and on about the revival. "Did you see Sharon Johnston? She was genuinely caught up in the spirit."

"Mrs. Daniels went forward for the very first time."

"And Tim, did you see him on the floor, under the spell of the Lord."

Shorty and I sat in silence. I felt strange there in the dark, like I was somehow disconnected from the people in the front seat, from the experience I'd just had at the church, from reality. When we finally pulled up in the driveway Dee's mother asked, "Sissy, how did it feel to get saved?"

The question startled me and my mind froze. Since I couldn't think of anything, I just kept quiet. I still felt slightly invisible sitting in the darkness holding my dog.

"We'll pick you up at seven again tomorrow night," Dee said, as I put my hand on the door handle.

A flash of fear charged through me as I stepped from the car and retreated quickly into the night. Shorty and I sat for a long time beneath the willows and watched the creek creatures play in the moonlight.

The evening replayed in my mind. Some parts of the experience had been fun and entertaining. I liked the excitement and passion of the church people and the way they got caught up in the sermon. At Grandmother's church, if you dared even rattle a paper, everyone turned to stare.

But thinking of the clutches of the giant preacher made me strip off my shoes and socks and stick my feet in the mud. Reliving the ride in the backseat of the car with Dee and her mother caused me to squirm out of my clothes and sit naked in the moonlight.

"You wanta go back tomorrow night?" I asked my dog.

"Errf," Shorty said, backing up and looking straight at me. "Errf, Errf."

"Me neither," I said, wondering exactly how I'd get out of it.

The next evening Dad happened to be off work when the car appeared in the driveway. I had no intention of returning to the church house, so I hadn't mentioned the fact that Dee and her mother would be stopping.

We'd eaten supper and Dad was doing a welding job in the shop. I edged around behind him when Dee and her mother walked into view of the yard lights.

"You ready, Sissy Gal?" Dee asked.

"Shorty and I don't want to go," I said, stepping out from behind my Dad.

"What do you say?" Dad was looking down at me.

"Thank you very much for asking."

Dee's mom approached us, and in a tone laced with velvet said to Dad, "Sissy and Shorty got saved last night, Mr. Jacobs. She NEEDS to go to church with us."

Dad looked at the lady then down at me. He shifted his feet around and laid his hammer on his workbench. "Sissy, you want to go?"

I shook my head with an emphatic, No.

"It's up to her. She doesn't want to go," Dad said.

"But, she NEEDS to go, Mr. Jacobs. You don't understand."

My dad reached and jerked up his hammer, his expression changed from friendliness to irritation. "No, ma'm, she doesn't NEED to do anything if she doesn't want to. Goodnight to you."

Dee and her mother walked a few steps, then stopped and discussed the situation in whispers, looking back at me, then shaking their heads in the dark shadows of the yard light. Finally they went to the car and drove away.

Their actions caused me to feel uncomfortable in a way I couldn't understand.

I helped Dad late into the evening, holding a piece of angle iron while he welded, handing him the hammer and wire brush. After awhile he stopped what he was doing, rolled a cigarette, stuck it in his lips, and lit it. Inhaling deeply, he flicked the ash in midair and let out a puff of smoke.

"So you didn't like their church?"

Dad was looking at me with that intensity that he sometimes had. One of his direct questions always made me nervous.

I squirmed, rubbing my bare ankles together. "Shorty and I liked parts of it." I admitted, not anxious to go into detail.

"What did you and Shorty get saved from?" He asked, looking down at me.

It was a question that had troubled me all day, but I still didn't have an honest answer. "I'm not rightly sure," I said in a puzzled tone.

My dad choked out a hearty laugh. He tossed back his head then and began to howl. He leaned on the workbench, shuddering with gasps of hooting laughter. I'd never seen him laugh so hard about anything in all of my life. Finally he slumped over onto his sawhorse and gave into the fit, leaning his head on the workbench and wiping slobber from his chin.

VII

One summer evening Dad made an announcement at supper that caused us kids to stop eating and stare at each other above our beans and corn bread.

"I'm taking Wildy to the sale tomorrow," Dad said, flatly. "The old fool keeps going through the fence and she's impossible to doctor. I've had it with her. It may take every one of us to get her up and loaded."

The animal Dad was referring to, Wildy, was a mixed Angus cow that was born on the farm and had been around as long as I could remember. She had, no doubt, received her name from my father. Dad tagged all of the farm animals with names. He'd often have a critter for the best part of a year before beginning to call them by a particular name. Us kids waited patiently for the new names to surface, often guessing and making bets ahead of time about the "christening."

Sometimes it would be a simple name such as Mot or Freckles because of appearance. But usually my father named his cows because of their personality, taking

great pains to study their character. "Mama Cow" because of a tendency to babysit all the herd calves. Or
"Miss Astor" when a certain cow seemed to take top
rung on the society ladder, bossing the other cows at
will.

Dad liked it when I'd corner him and ask why he
named a particular animal. "Why did you name her
'Hypo'?" I would always wait until we were alone and I
knew he wasn't too busy, because of the pure enjoy-
ment Dad got from his long-winded explanations.

My father would usually stop his welding or fence
building, take his tobacco and papers from his overalls
pocket, and begin to roll a cigarette as he explained.
"Well, you see, she's a born hypochondriac."

"What's hypochondriac mean?" I'd climb up on the
workbench or corner post to listen more closely.

"Well, it's someone who's sick all of the time or at
least thinks they are. Some people have one ailment
right after the other, always whining, but most of their
problems are just in the head."

Dad's explanation for the names were an education
and always intrigued me. "So how do you know she
complains all the time? Does she talk to you the way
Shorty talks to me?"

"In a way she does just that," Dad said, flashing his
handsome smile. "If she gets off her feed she's telling
me she's got a belly ache. She walks the fence row in a
nervous fit, telling me she's worrying about something.
She's never normal. Never just an ordinary, grazing
cow contented to be alive."

That evening at the table, when Dad made the announcement about selling Wildy, four pair of feet

bumped gently back and forth into each other beneath the bench where we sat side by side. It was our silent form of communication. We hated to see Wildy go.

Dad told everyone Wildy was a "half-bubble off square," but I could never quite determine whether the black cow was mean-hearted, incredibly smart, or truly crazy.

If I was in the pasture chasing butterflies or grass-hoppers, she would act real nonchalant like the other cows. Grazing away, she would not even cast a glance my way. But when I least expected it, a thundering tor-nado would shake the ground and I'd look up to see a storming black blur headed right for me.

Wildy had no regard for size, authority, or numbers. She had her turn chasing every one of us, including Mama and Dad.

Finally, in self-defense, us kids decided one day to get even. We ganged up on her, the four of us circling closely with sticks, yelling obscenities and driving her into a mad fit. What started out to be a onetime session of getting even, then turned into a game.

We called it Wild Cow and oftentimes, when some-one spent the night, we'd introduce them to our brand of country entertainment. Forming a circle and holding a rag in one hand, stick in the other, we'd walk up to Wildy, shouting and flapping our rags. The poor cow would wait, usually until we were all within twenty feet, acting as if she didn't even see us.

Her "circus act" was well worth the wait. She would begin to throw her head from side to side, dark eyes glazing with a demon gold, then she'd jump straight in the air and come down in a furious spin like a bull in a rodeo. Round and round she'd go, faster and faster until she'd nearly fall down. When she'd stop, her legs would spraddle apart and she'd be slobbering with rage. Whoever she focused on first became her target.

When Wildy started her charge at one of us, the others immediately ran toward her shaking rags, rattling sticks and hollering so that she became confused and gave up the attack on that particular victim. Sometimes she bounded immediately toward another one of us which kept the game interesting. We'd repeat the process until she stood, frothing and stumbling, too tired to chase.

It was great sport and never failed to entertain the neighbor kids and especially anyone who came from the city. We were always very cautious to make sure Dad was in town at work so we wouldn't get caught.

Sometimes, when we all felt especially reckless, we'd each contribute a nickel to the game and whoever got close enough to actually touch Wildy without getting attacked in return won the pot of money. On one such occasion, Bub, trying to show off in front of Carolyn, almost earned himself a trip to the hospital.

Wildy lifted her head after spinning and took after Carolyn. Bub bounced in to save the day, running between Carolyn and Wildy. The cow spun. Bub grabbed her tail and for a few hilarious moments my older brother was attached to the cow, hollering and bouncing as Wildy spun around and around.

Unfortunately for Bub, he tripped, fell down, and before we could go in for a rescue, Wildy mauled him good with her head, butting him into the ground and stomping over him as she kicked away.

We carried Bub, unconscious, to the creek where he slowly came to life. He had two black eyes, his lip was split, and ribs bruised. Sis was excited about calling Dad with the first emergency, but Bub refused to let us summon Dad from work. That evening we concocted a story about him falling from the loft in a game of King on the Mountain.

Dad examined my brother's wounds and looked at us all with tired eyes. I'm sure by his long sigh he didn't believe the King on the Mountain story, but he didn't seem to have the energy to pursue the conversation.

Mama was living on the farm with us the day Dad planned to haul Wildy to the sale. I sensed her amusement at the breakfast table that morning.

"How do you expect to get Wildy up?" Mama asked, a look of humor in her expression.

"We'll figure out a way," Dad snapped. "The only reason I haven't done it before now is the bother of it. But her crazy ways are becoming more bother than taking her to the sale. It'll probably take the better part of a morning and every one of us to get it done." His frown turned slowly into a grand smile. "Of course, some lucky fool will get a heck of a bargain, won't he?"

We all laughed. My feelings were mixed between relief and sorrow. I always hated to say good-bye to one of our farm animals and teasing Wildy had become our favorite game to show company. But it would be a relief to play in the pasture without always looking over my shoulder in fear.

So Dad started laying out his plan after breakfast. "Sis, you get on Maybelle and the rest of us will go on

Lou Dean

foot. Everyone carry a stick. You know how Wildy can be. If we herd all of the cows toward the barn, we'll pen as many as it takes to get her in the corral. Let's move slow now, no running and wild screaming or they'll all get upset and we won't accomplish anything."

Bub and Lil Bub and I formed a close trio, because we all had a healthy respect for Wildy's attack abilities. Sis started riding Maybelle along the far south fence line where most of the cows were grazing that morning. The rest of us walked along behind on foot, moving silently as the cows sauntered along in the general direction of the barn.

Wildy was at first clustered into the middle of things, but all at once, as if she suddenly sensed danger, the black head begin to swing from side to side. She spun, reared, then took off in a dead run toward the east end of the farm.

Mama, who was bringing up the eastern edge of our line, hollered and waved her stick at Wildly in a futile attempt to stop the escape. The cow jumped the creek, almost ran over Mama and tore out like a coonhound on the scent, taking a dozen cows with her.

"Why didn't you stop her?" Dad bellowed at Mama.

My mother stared at Dad with fiery eyes. "If I had taken one more step she would have run right over the top of me," Mama screamed back.

"I know what that feels like," Bub whispered to me and we both grinned.

Two hours later we had regrouped. With a slow sweep of the south pasture, we gathered the bulk of the herd and had them bawling from the barnyard. Dad's philosophy was that Wildy and the others would come easier once they saw their companions in the corral.

But Wildy had a different idea of how things were going to go. She was thoroughly riled by then, and once Wildy's temper had been ruffled, she pulled out her best tricks. With eyes alert, she blasted out of the small group of remaining cows each time we began to gather them. Always, one or two of her comrades would follow. Tails high, they bolted off past one of us into the timber east of the barn and the other cows would scatter like marbles.

Each time it was the same scene. Dad would holler out to the guilty party, "Damn it, why didn't you stop her? That's why you have that stick in your hand, isn't it?"

During each rampage all of us except Mama remained silent. She usually managed a few words that sent Dad further into his rage.

"Probably they didn't want to commit suicide today."

Finally, hours later, Wildy and three remaining cows crowded into a small bunch and were slowly approaching the gate. The four animals meandered down the soft dust of the path, past the pigpen, the water trough, and hesitated a few feet before they reached the corral gate.

Dad signaled frantically for Lil Bub to open the gate and stand back, and for the rest of us to close in. One cow saw the opening and dived toward her bawling companions, eager to be with the others. A second followed willingly as we closed in tighter toward Wildy and her remaining friend.

Wildy's eyes glazed and she lowered her head when she realized she was almost trapped. Spinning, she turned and faced Dad head on. My father raised his stick, his thick fingers secure around the two-inch-thick weapon.

"Get on in there," he roared.

Wildy reared into her circus act, coming down in a spin. She dived right toward Dad who bashed her between the horns. The black cow twirled back into her spin, catching Dad on the shoulder with her right hip, ejecting him ten feet backward into the creek. Bucking and twisting, the victorious cow disappeared back into the blackjack thicket.

"I'm gonna kill that bitch," Dad said, standing with water dripping from his scarlet face.

I was holding my breath, straining every blood vessel not to laugh. Behind me I heard Bub calmly clearing his throat with controlled little "hurmmps" while Sis coughed gently behind her hand.

It was Mama who lost control. She let out a burst of breath, like she was blowing out a clump of candles on a cake. "Why didn't you stop her?" she asked, offering Dad a hand from the bank. The words barely made it out before the laughter bubbled from deep in her throat. Violent spasms of laughter jerked from my mother and she bent and held her sides as the gaiety rolled out. Sis and Bub joined in and I was surely relieved to help.

Dad walked dripping from the creek. "It wasn't that damned funny," he said stomping off toward the house. His words sent all of us into a whole new fit.

Dad returned in a few minutes, carrying his double-barreled shotgun. "Come on," he said with a growl.

"He wouldn't ..." I whispered to Mama.

Mama looked at me. "Oh no, don't worry. He's just hopping mad and needed some kind of reinforcement. He may scare her with it, but he wouldn't shoot her. She's worth too much."

The words quieted my fears. Mama knew Dad pretty well. I'd never seen him mad enough to let his temper interfere with his ability to cling to a dollar. But one thing was certain in my mind. The cow had met her match. My father would not quit until Wildy was in the corral. I let out an exhausted sigh.

An hour later, we had Wildy and her Hereford friend approaching the gate again. I saw Dad hesitate by the water trough and push two fat shells into his gun. I was afraid what might happen if Wildly and my father lost their tempers a second time. It was hard to have a deep attachment to the mean cow, but I didn't want to watch her get shot.

Dad motioned for Lil Bub to open the gate. All of us closed in slowly. This time the Hereford was in front. She took one look at the open gate and ran in. She'd had enough excitement for one morning and was probably tired of running.

Wildy was right at her heels, head down as if she were going on through. Before she had time to hesitate or have second thoughts, "Bam!" Dad fired the old shotgun into the air just behind Wildy's flank. All of us jumped, including Wildy, who then found herself trapped inside the corral.

"Ha!" Dad screamed in victory. "Gotcha." Slamming and latching the gate, he broke down his gun, retrieved the empty shells, then looked at his watch. "Let's go have a bite to eat, then we'll get Miss Wildy loaded for the sale."

It was a silent sandwich. Dad was still in no mood for conversation. Twice, Bub nudged me under the table with his foot and made a funny face, but he didn't get a giggle out of me. He was trying to set me up for murder and I knew it. Dad was definitely not in the mood for foolishness. As I swallowed my cheese sandwich and washed it down with milk, I had no ambition for the long afternoon ahead.

"OK," Dad said, back at the corral. "This is what we'll do." A confident calmness had returned to his voice. He took the last draw from his cigarette, dropped it into the dust, and ground it with the toe of his brogan boot.

"Bub, you and Sissy Gal can operate the gate that goes to the chute. Just stand and pay attention. The rest of us are going to mill around in the corral until we get Wildy positioned just right here." He took his arms and held them in a V-shape in the air, walking a few feet in front of the rickety gate that led to the cattle chute. "When I holler 'Open' you two fling the gate wide and the rest of us will push her in. The second you see her go past, get that gate closed."

I looked at Bub and felt a shudder on the inside. I would have preferred a different job. The old gate was heavy and wobbly. If you weren't careful it could twist on its hinges and flop you around like a fish on a line. I always hated being stationed on the gate during such episodes. I knew from long experience around my father, if anything went wrong, the gate person was first to get blamed.

But my older brother gave a quick nod of confidence toward Dad and winked at me. "This oughta be interestin," he whispered.

"Now, it's going to take time," Dad said, his tone even and patient. "We don't dare open the corral gate and try to weed out some of these other cows. Chances are they'd get to running and she'd be the first one out. So we have a lot of animals here to deal with. Be careful, watch yourselves, don't get mashed or kicked."

The cows milled nervously around the perimeter of the corral fence, bawling and shitting. There were thirty-some head, mostly Hereford and a few Angus crossbreeds. Fortunately, Wildy was the only solid black cow, so she was easy to spot.

Dad motioned for Mama, Sis, and Lil Bub to man their sticks and form a half-circle. They began to move in. Slowly, Dad would maneuver Wildy, crowded among a few companions, in the general vicinity of the chute gate. But the demented cow seemed to have a premonition about what was happening and eyed the gate with great apprehension. She'd been tricked through one gate which resulted in close confinement of the barnyard. She had no intention of negotiating a second.

Once, Dad and his group got Wildy close enough to taste victory. "Open it," Dad screamed.

I jerked on my end of the gate, lifting and running backward with every fiber in my gut. A huge crowd of

cattle bombarded past Bub and me, penning us between the gate and the barn. I stood breathless, ready
to run forward and shut the gate, but Dad's command
didn't come.

"Damn it all to hell. You loco, brainless bitch." He
walked over and herded the dozen or more cows back
out of the chute and motioned for us to close our gate.
Wildy had run past Lil Bub at the last minute.

Hours passed. The July sun beat relentlessly down
in the barnyard. Fat green flies stuck to my arms and
bit at the back of my neck. The stench from the accu-
mulating cow piles baked up a reeking odor in the afternoon heat. Dad's earlier optimism began to wane.

"Bub," Dad squalled, after yet another futile attempt. "You can handle that gate alone, can't you?"

"Yes sir," Bub replied, throwing back his shoulders.
My brother at twelve was not big, but like Dad, he was
strong and wiry for his size.

"Sissy, you get on out here. What we need is just
one more hand. You stick near your little brother and if
that bitch starts toward you, both of you scream, wave
your hands, jump, and swing those sticks. Don't let her
get by."

Working my way through the mass of bawling,
stinking cows, I suddenly wished to be back with Bub
behind the safety of the gate. But, on the next pass,
Wildy became tangled right in the center of a bunch of
cows that seemed anxious to stampede through the
gate that Bub threw open. The cows both in front and
behind Wildy bolted toward the opening and she was
shoved totally against her will through the wobbly gate
into the chute area.

Bub put his shoulder into his task, pushing the lump of cows on in and squealed out with satisfaction as he latched the gate.

"Ahh," Dad said. "Good job, lad. We've got her now."

After another thirty minutes of similar frustrations, Wildy was alone in the chute penned tightly with posts wedged in front and behind her at several levels to keep her held in place.

Dad backed the old pickup snug against the mouth of the chute and stood sizing up the situation for several minutes while we all waited.

Wildy's eyes were livid. She tossed her head back and forth casting snot in four directions as she bounced forward and backward, up and down, like a wild bull in a bucking chute trying to dislodge his rider.

Getting her into the pickup was not the biggest challenge. The stock racks on back of the truck were built with a gate that swung from left to right instead of sliding up and down. This meant that we had to get Wildy on down the chute, in the truck, and then, in order to secure the gate, the pickup had to be pulled forward several feet away from the chute.

"Johnnie Lou, you get in the truck," Dad said to my mother. "When I holler 'Go' you pull forward as fast as you can so we can get that gate shut on the stock racks."

Mama had a look of complete conformity on her face, but there was just a hint of amusement in her lifted eyebrows. "I'll do my best. Let's hope that's good enough."

Dad ignored the sarcasm and continued with his orders. "Keep the engine running, your foot on the clutch, and the truck in first gear. We may not have but a few seconds to get the gate shut, so be ready."

As Mama crawled in the truck and fired it up, I was relieved I didn't have her job. The timing on this maneuver was going to be crucial. One thing was certain at this point, Wildy was not stupid. The second she turned and saw that open gate on the stock racks, she'd jump.

"Sis, you're the tallest, so you stay on the ground. Stand off to the side with your hands on that stock rack gate. The second your mother pulls the truck forward, slam it shut. I may be in there with the crazy bitch. That doesn't matter. You understand? Your job is to shut the gate, no matter where I am."

Sis took her position and nervously wrapped her fingers around the sucker rod gate, shifting her weight so she'd be ready to put her back into the task.

"OK, Sissy, you will be on the posts. Stand outside of the chute and when I tell you 'Pull' jerk those front two posts out so we can drive her forward into the pickup."

I stepped to the side of the chute and placed my hands on the upper post. Wildy's head was wagging just a few feet from my face, sending her saliva into my eyes and across my neck. Being that close to her rolling eyeballs was unsettling, but I told myself she couldn't get to me.

"Bub, you back me up. When Sissy pulls those posts out, Wildy only has two directions she can go. Up or forward. We want forward. I want you to stand overhead with your stick. When I start hollering and hitting her rump, you keep your eye on her. If she even looks like she might jump over, you start whacking her with everything you've got."

Bub climbed to his post, centering himself above Wildy. He was in a grand mood and obviously enjoying the entire project. He looked down at me, winked, and began to whistle "Yankee Doodle."

Wildy, who had a particular dislike for Bub, began to throttle from side to side banging her body hard, testing the strength of Dad's chute.

Dad climbed behind the cow. He had replaced his earlier tree limb with half a fence post. It had been a long, exhausting day and he meant business.

"OK, everyone ready?"

"Ready," Mama replied above the roar of the pickup.

"Ready," Sis said, tightening her grasp on the stock rack gate.

"I'm ready," I agreed, both of my hands on posts.

"Let's do it," Bub said from above.

"OK, Sissy. PULL."

I yanked the posts, first the upper then lower with two quick motions, expecting all hell to break loose above me.

Dad was mashing the sharp edge of his broken fence post into Wildy's rump, but she wouldn't budge. "Come on, you contrary ..." Dad put his weight into it, his solid frame and thick muscular shoulders grinding the jagged post into the cow's butt.

Wildy grunted and her head became suddenly still. She folded her legs and crashed to the floor of the chute. As she went down, she gave a quick flip of her shitty tail and caught Dad right across the face.

Dad's head snapped, whipped back by the wet green slime that smacked him between the eyes. He dropped his weapon. The motion of Wildy's body going down jammed the broken post up, catching Dad between the legs.

My father fell with a moan, grabbing his crotch and rolling unconcerned in the mess of cow shit that covered the chute floor.

"Put your posts back, Sissy. In case she gets up ... before Dad does." Bub had a hard time keeping a straight face.

I quickly obeyed and kept in position, waiting.

Mama and Sis couldn't see the action from where they were, so both of them waited, patient and ready for several more minutes.

Dad emerged. His face beneath the green was white and there was a calm but killing resolve in his eyes. He climbed out of the chute very slowly and walked over next to me.

"Sissy, run over there in the garden and fetch the hoe."

When I returned, Dad took the handle of the hoe and shoved it through the boards of the chute, thrusting Wildy in the flank with vicious, quick jabs. "Get up, you ... ignorant, unscrupulous, baffling witch." Dad prodded her with each word.

At first, the wild cow seemed determined to ignore the attack. She stayed in her crumpled position, legs under her, head resting nicely on the boards beneath her. But when Dad's punching became an assault of thumping pain that radiated through her entire hind quarters, Wildy responded. With the speed of a wolf, she gathered herself and jumped straight up in the air.

Wildy's feet were paddling just in front of Bub's face and my brother was pounding on Wildy's head, trying to duck at the same time.

"Keep her in there," Dad roared. Jumping back in the chute, he brought the heavy post bashing down on the cow's back.

"Pull your posts, Sissy," Dad screamed. His red hair was jutting out like the great mane of a lion, his eyes now bronzed with determination.

I jerked my posts. Wildy lunged forward, clearing the remaining three feet of the chute and crashed into the truck. Scrambling quickly around, she started to jump out the inviting open gate of the stock racks. Dad roared. Bringing his post down right on Wildy's nose, he jumped into the bed of the pickup with her, defying her to move him.

The cow put her head down and bashed toward my father. "Noooo" he squalled, catching the blow full in the chest.

Mama, who'd been anxiously waiting her command from the pickup, mistook the scream for "Go." She jerked the old truck quickly away from the chute with Sis swinging from the stock rack gate.

The motion threw Wildy and Dad forward spiraling out of the back of the pickup into a tangled heap on the ground. Instantly, the wild cow jumped up. Slinging her head in triumph, she farted and kicked away, bucking and twisting with freedom. When she reached the creek she paused to have a luxurious long drink, glanced back at us, then took off in a dead run for the far pasture.

Dad didn't react for several moments. Mama got out of the truck and walked back. She had no idea what had happened, but was wise enough not to ask.

"Dean, you OK?" she said, meekly, kneeling next to my father.

Poor Dad was covered from head to foot with shit. He had it in his hair, streaked across his face, dried on his eyelashes, and it blended nicely across the front of his overalls with the mud he'd received earlier that morning.

Us kids stood several feet back expecting the worst. Dad finally stood up, slowly. He moved his upper body around, swiveling his hips in an attempt to see if anything was broken. Making a fist with his right hand, he pivoted it in a little circle.

"Actually," he said, "I think I am."

My father didn't start his usual tirade of accusations as to why the mission failed. He didn't yell at Mama for misreading her cue. He took several limping steps toward the house then stopped.

"I think Wildy wants to remain part of this family," he said, struggling for just the right words. "It seems to be important to her. What do you all think?"

Everyone agreed with silent, smirking nods.

"Well," Dad said, in his attempt to salvage what little dignity he had left, "If it means that much to her, I believe I'll let her stay."

VIII

Exasperating was a word I learned in third grade vocabulary. The moment I found its meaning in the worn, school dictionary, I grinned. It would be an easy one to remember because it was a synonym for my older brother.

Bub had a knack for recognizing the very thing that bothered a person most and loved to use that information to provoke a reaction. He had a sharp mind, which aided him in these endeavors, and he made it his mission in life to become an accomplished irritation.

During the summer months when we went into Ponca City to buy groceries, Dad would sometimes let each of us kids pick two bottles of sparkling soda pop to take home and drink at our leisure. I always loved Grapette. No matter how hard I tried to stretch the pleasure of my two treasured bottles, I usually drank both pops within the first week. Sis loved Coke and Lil Bub orange and they had even less discipline than I. Their sodas were gone the first two or three days.

Bub would save his soda until the hottest days of the entire summer, after all the rest of us had devoured ours, then he'd make the announcement.

"It's a perfect summer day for a cold soda pop." He'd pull one of his two bottles of Dr. Pepper out from some hiding place, put it in the freezer until it was half-frozen, then bring it out and sip it slowly in front of everyone. He'd savor each slushy swallow, churning it around in his mouth, then smiling as he'd burp. "Sorry you drank yours. I'll give you a sip for a quarter." He'd repeat the entire process a day or so later with the second pop.

My brother was always trying to corner everyone into a bet. "Betcha I can spit from here to that fence post, over the top wire." When I was very young, he was able to squeeze every penny of my allowance by such maneuvers because I was naive and didn't realize he had always practiced before he would wager.

As time passed, however, I became wise of Bub's tricks and refused to listen when he approached me. Unfortunately, Lil Bub was still young and stupid. Even though I'd warned him that Bub only bet on sure things, my little brother was as gullible as I had once been.

The neighbor kids and any company who visited the farm were true targets for my brother's games. On any given week, between school and home, Bub could always sucker a few quarters. My brother would buy penny candy at the Nine Mile Corner and go to school with his overalls pockets bulging. He'd generously sell it to anyone who was interested for a nickel a piece.

When the teacher assigned each student in fourth grade to have a bug collection for biology, my brother told Lil Bub and me to pick up various beatles, locusts, and butterflies when we saw them on the farm. He, in turn, sold them to fourth graders for a quarter each. Bub's ventures finally earned him a less than desirable reputation among the teachers.

When Bub left Braden School to attend eighth grade in Ponca City, he left me an unwanted legacy. The principal hated my brother.

Although I couldn't completely fault Mrs. B. for that, I didn't feel it fair for me to inherit her leftover wrath. But as luck would have it, she took an instant dislike to me and I squirmed beneath her appraising eye each day. After a full year of false accusations against me, harsh punishments, and an attitude of complete distrust, I began to tire of trying to impress Mrs. B with my kind heart and good intentions.

About that same time, when I was in fifth grade, something strange began to take place. Mrs. B suddenly had a change of heart. One afternoon she offered to let me and Carolyn go outside during class and dust the erasers, a job usually assigned to one of her three "pets."

"Has she ever let you dust the erasers before?" I asked Carolyn as we smacked the felt board erasers together sending yellow dust out into the wind.

"Are you kidding? I'm YOUR best friend. She doesn't like me."

"Wonder what's come over her?"

Then the very next afternoon, she appointed me monitor of the cloakroom for the week. It was a position I'd longed to have for an entire year. Every time she asked for a volunteer, I'd wave frantically from the back of the room and she'd ignore me. Why had she suddenly come right out and offered the job to me?

Bub solved the mystery of Mrs. B's personality change the next day while we were picking beans in the garden.

"I can't figure what's come over teacher," I said and began to tell my brother of the change.

Bub stood up and let out a howl of laughter.

"What is it?"

"Politics," he said, grinning. "Yes, that's my old buddy, Mrs. B. Always eager to please the school board."

"What are you talkin about, Bub?"

"It's Dad. They elected him president of the school board at the P.T.A. meeting last Friday night. He didn't really want it, but they all talked him into it, saying it was his turn."

"What's that mean, president of the school board?"

"Well, you see, Sissy, Dad now has the authority to hire and fire the teachers. In other words, your friend and mine, Mrs. B is afraid to lay a hand on you because if ... just if she were to rile Dad, she could lose her job."

Bub laughed again, bending over the row of green beans. "Oh yes, I wish I was back in her room. I'd have me some real fun."

Lil Bub came walking up about that time with a cigar box. He popped the lid back. "Lookey what I got?" He set the box on the ground and stuck his fingers inside, allowing a huge brown tarantula to climb up his sleeve.

I stepped back. "Gee, Lil Bub, aren't you afraid that thing will bite you?"

"Herman won't bite. He's got personality."

"Where'd you get him?" Bub said, stepping closer and examining our little brother's find.

"Down by the granary near the creek. He was just crawlin along the gravel road as pretty as you please. Ain't he grand?"

Bub put his fingers up near Lil Bub's shoulder and the big spider willingly detoured over to Bub's arm where he traveled up and around my older brother's neck.

"You want him, Sissy?" Bub said, stepping closer to me.

"No thanks," I said, taking several steps back. I suppose because we'd been taking about teacher, I added, "I feel about like Mrs. B does, the only good spider is a dead one."

Something lit up in Bub's face, an amazing flash of light streaked first in his eyes then glowed with a blush on his cheeks.

"Sissy," he said. "I've got a good joke on Mrs. B. It's a way you could get even with her for all the mean things she's done to you."

I started shaking my head. I knew what Bub was thinking, but I had three more years at Braden. Dad being on the school board might make some difference, but I wasn't willing to gamble with my life.

"Come on, Sissy," Bub said, handing the fuzzy spider back to Lil Bub.

"You could take it in for Show and Tell. Mrs. B always loves it when someone brings something. You could just accidently stumble on the way to the front of the class and toss Herman on her desk."

Lil Bub was listening and started shaking his head. "No, I don't want anything to happen to Herman."

"Maybe you could go along, Lil Bub. You know how teacher lets you come in the late afternoon sometimes and sit by Sissy. You could go along and watch the fun. Protect your spider. He won't get hurt."

Bub reached in his pocket and drew out his wad of dollar bills. "I'll give you each a dollar."

I stared at him in disbelief. He wanted to scare Mrs. B in the worst way. My brother never offered me money. I thought for a moment about the personality change in the teacher and wondered just how much I could get away with. I was tired of her taking her frustrations out on me.

"Five dollars." I said, amazed that I had enough nerve to spit the words out.

Bub laughed. "No way, Sissy. No way."

"No deal then," I said, bending over the beans.

"Two," Bub said.

I stood up and thought about how many times my brother had won my allowance money with his stupid bets. How many soda pops he'd sipped in front of me, charging me a quarter a drink. How many times I'd collected bugs and terrapins and other things that he later sold.

"Five."

Bub rolled out five ones, grinning. "You drive a hard bargain, Sister. Under one condition."

"What?"

"You come and tell me every detail after it happens. I want to hear it all."

"OK." I took the five ones and Lil Bub reluctantly took his one dollar bill.

The day before I took Herman to school, I set things in motion. I had a written permission note for Lil Bub to join me in class last hour. Since he'd be in kindergarten the next year, Mrs. B permitted him to visit sometimes. I'd also made the announcement that I had a project for Show and Tell during that time period.

Bringing something for Show and Tell included offering information to the class, so I'd done my research and had my paper. I didn't want teacher to suspect any foul play if anything went amiss.

"That'll be fine, Sissy." Mrs. B smiled on Monday morning. "You always have such interesting things from your farm."

The teacher's praise toward me was so unusual, I looked at her twice to make sure I'd heard her right. The compliment gave me new courage for my plan. I smiled and flashed Mrs. B my innocent look.

The next afternoon, with Lil Bub sitting securely beside my desk, the teacher called on me. I took the cigar box slowly from my younger brother.

"What kind of wonderful surprise does Miss Lou Dean have for us in that little box?" teacher sang. For one fleeting moment I had a spark of guilt, but there was no time now for second thoughts.

Spiders were things of disgust to Mrs. B. When she'd see one hanging from the ceiling or streaking

across the floor of the schoolhouse, she'd immediately
stop what she was doing and run for the broom. With
an attack that bordered on hysteria, she'd whack at the
innocent creeper and wouldn't stop until the poor spider was flattened.

"Squash it. Step on it," she'd scream, if the intruder
evaded her broom. Thirty little feet would then slap relentlessly across the hardwood floor until a scream of
triumph would hail victory. Then, she'd have someone
hold the dustpan while she scooped the dead body in
with the broom. The wastebasket was an inappropriate
place to dispose of the body. She wanted a volunteer to
take the corpse outside and fling it back behind the
building.

Even I wasn't afraid of granddaddy long legs, but
when we tried to point out to Mrs. B that those spiders
were harmless, she ignored our pleas and proceeded
with her usual ritual. During these "spider sessions" everything came to a screeching halt until the offender
was whisked away outside, out of her sight.

My chair screeched slowly against the floor as I
stood. I had given the plan a great deal of thought. I
would accidently stumble on the way to the front of the
class and Herman would just happen to end up on
teacher's desk. In case things didn't go well and she
told Dad, I could claim innocence to the very end.
They'd never know for sure.

I had told my little brother about teacher's fear of
spiders and the strict ritual for murder she always followed. He knew he had only a few seconds after the

scare to gather Herman and get him safely in the cigar box.

Just as I started toward the front, Mrs. B stood and walked away from her desk. My mind spun with new possibilities and I quickly decided I had only one choice. I had to hurl Herman through the air and pray that he landed on target. With three fast steps, I faked my stumble and Herman went flying.

Mrs. B happened to have on a loose knitted dress that came to my aid. Herman landed just below teacher's waist and clung to the dress like a locust shell to a tree trunk.

For one horrible second, everyone froze. Herman clung, Mrs. B stared, I stood. Then Herman, insecure in his new environment, began to travel up. He was a fast mover and with a great burst of speed, tickled past teacher's bosom, up her shoulders, around her neck to the top of her twisted bun of braided hair.

Before Mrs. B was able to kick her body into motion, strange, feeble noises erupted from her throat. Bubbling gurgles of despair choked from her gaping mouth and saliva splattered down her chin. Her eyes turned an interesting shade of yellow and all other color drained from her face.

Then Herman, suddenly confronted with the end of his road, turned and abruptly started his journey back. The feathery sensation of his great legs on Mrs. B's hair sent her into spasms. She leaned forward at the waist and began to bounce like someone going down the sidewalk playing hopscotch. Round and around she banged her feet, whisking at her hair with both hands, sending little combs and bobby pens bouncing to the hardwood floor.

When her hair was hanging in a great long heap, she threw her body backward so that she was standing, then she began to jump, scratch, and shake. Like Elvis singing "Jailhouse Rock," teacher swiveled and shook until the entire class was roaring with laughter.

The commotion finally dislodged poor Herman who went flying across the room and landed near the blackboard. "Kill it. Kill it!" Mrs. B squalled.

Lil Bub was already out of his chair and to the rescue, just in time to scoop his spider into the box before ten slamming feet stomped his pet into oblivion.

Mrs. B was trembling all over. Her long hair waved down her back and sweat formed little beads across her fat face. Her eyes latched onto mine.

"It was an accident," I said, when she took a step toward me. Her shaking fingers were coming for my neck.

"DAD," I said, real loud. "DAD thought it was a good idea for me to bring the spider. He suggested it." I lied, knowing I was very close to extinction.

The words somehow registered into the teacher's muddled brain and she stopped, two inches from my throat. She kept looking at me, trembling, then she turned slowly and crept to her desk, collapsing in a great lump.

"You ... you may ..." Her jaws were opening and shutting in strange little attempts to speak, but the words somehow wouldn't form. Finally she grabbed the bell in one trembling hand and it ding, ding, dinged in her quaking fingers.

Lil Bub and I were the first ones out the door.

That evening when Bub was down feeding his pigs, I told him. He sat on his five-gallon slop bucket and held his sides as he howled. I stood and reenacted Mrs. B's shaking and jumping, flipping over at the waist and whipping at my hair, then I reached my shaking hands out for my brother's neck.

Bub laughed until tears rolled down his face. "Oh, Sissy, that's the funniest thing I've ever heard. I'd have given my bone-handled corn knife to have seen it." His laughter echoed out over the creek and bounced back into my ears, making me grin.

When I finally turned to walk away, Bub said, "Oh, Sissy, about my five dollars."

I stopped dead still and turned.

"If you'll give it back to me now, I won't tell Dad that you're intentionally taking advantage of poor Mrs. B just because he's on the school board."

He said the words real serious, but I saw a flash of gaiety flick across his blue eyes.

"Eat dirt," I said.

My brother erupted into another full tirade of hooting howls.

IX

Spring in Oklahoma meant storms. In March the winds started bringing great, gray clouds that came from four directions and seemed to clash right above Osage County.

Sometimes I would sit in the cellar and try to understand what God was doing above us. Was He in a bad mood because of the long winter and this was His way of shrugging off the blues? Maybe the devil was challenging His territory and God had unleashed His wrath. When I would talk of my imaginings Bub would usually laugh and say, "It's spring in Oklahoma, Sissy. Don't complicate it."

Day after day the winds blasted across the hills bringing moist air rumbling in with deafening thunder and lightning that turned darkness into dawn. Hail the size of golf balls would hammer the trees and buildings and thump down on the critters relentlessly. Broken tree limbs, green leaves, shattered bark covered the wet ground from March until May.

At school, we'd spend at least one day a week crammed into the cellar, playing games in the semi-darkness while the teachers peeked out cautiously at the ominous sky.

When Mama was home, we spent half of our lives in the cellar because she was terrified of tornados. At the first threat of black clouds or rising wind, our mother would shuffle us all off into the dark hole just beyond the front steps of our house. After Mama left the farm, we seldom went to the cellar, because in the evenings Dad was usually in Ponca City at work. Sis was in charge while Dad worked and she dearly loved to sleep while it was storming. She could curl up in her quilts and sleep through the worst storm in history. The old wind could hammer, the rain could pound against the house, and the thunder vibrate the walls, but Sis wouldn't wake up.

Not going to the cellar was a relief to me. I hated the endless hours of waiting in the darkness of the stuffy hole. My favorite place during a storm was the barn. I would hoist Shorty up with me into the loft and sit sandwiched between warm bales of hay watching lightning flash and tree limbs fall, listening to the wind whistle through the cracks. I loved to see the trickle of a creek churn into a brown river crashing and frothing around the barn, snaking its way behind our house with a passion to reach some unknown destiny.

From late March until May we kept the kerosine lamps filled and the flashlights handy because the storms left us without electricity nearly every day. We boiled water for baths and to do dishes, went to bed at sundown, and arose at dawn.

After the storms leveled off, we always had lots of work to do picking up tree limbs, repairing roofs, and starting the spring planting. May was always one of my favorite times, a busy buzz of days with wildflowers blooming, tree blossoms ablaze with color, and the creek alive with mysterious guests.

The creek in early spring was the center of our social life. We fished, seined, swam in it, carried our food out next to it for picnics, slept by it at night. The swollen stream coming from the Arkansas River held a certain magic below its murky surface. It offered us mystery, excitement, and unlimited imaginary games. More than a dozen varieties of fish frequented its depth, as well as giant, soft-shelled turtles, bullfrogs and snakes, while dragonflies, barn swallows and water spiders skimmed its surface.

One bright Saturday in May when the air was throbbing with the sweetness of spring, Bub came up with an idea that filled Lil Bub and me with excitement. My younger brother and I had finished up our morning chores and were lingering near the rolling creek catching tadpoles.

Bub came swaggering up toward us carrying his old corn knife in one hand and a piece of paper in another. He had a patch of burlap tied over one eye with a baling twine and a large hoop ring of copper wire dangling from one ear.

"Hey, ye land lubbers," he hollered, waving the long-bladed knife. "Up with ya and let's be off to sea. Man the boat."

Lil Bub giggled and I just stared. It had been awhile since my older brother had been in a playing mood.

"What boat?" Lil Bub asked. "What's that paper in your hand, Bub?"

"The raft we're fixin to build," Bub said, grinning. He rustled the paper in his hand, folded it, and stuck it in his overalls. Patting his pocket he said, "So we can go find the buried treasure."

Ten minutes later, my brother had Lil Bub running to the barn for baling twine while I helped him gather up fence posts from around the shop. I didn't ask too many questions. It was a treat for Bub to play with us and he didn't like a lot of talk while he was working.

We lined up ten of those wooden posts and bound them tight together with twine. "These are good things for you to learn," Bub said, standing to admire the job. "In case you get stranded on an island sometime."

"What's an island?" Lil Bub asked.

"It's a piece of ground surrounded by water, Lil Bub."

"What if you don't have any posts or twine?"

Bub stared at our little brother. "Then you use your imagination. You cut small trees and bark to bind em."

"What if you don't have a knife?"

Bub ignored the bothersome question. He motioned for me to pick up one end of the raft. When I did, the posts shifted slightly, causing the flat surface to waffle up.

"It would be better if we could take us a post and lay one on the bottom and nail these others to it," he said, scratching his head and walking around the raft.

"How're you gonna find nails and a hammer on an island?" Lil Bub continued the interrogation. "And Dad will switch us if we nail into those fence posts."

Bub smiled a stretchy grin. "You have a point, little brother. Actually you have two points. We'll just rough it, make it work."

"Ain't those posts gonna roll and slide if we try standin on em in the water?" Lil Bub asked.

"Oh, maybe a little," Bub said, curling his lip. "But what kind of pirates are we anyway? Are we scared or are we MEAN?" He drew back his lip, pulled his patch back over his eye.

"Mean," Lil Bub hollered. "Let's go." He took his shirt off and hung it on the fence, then kneeling down he rolled up his breech legs to the knees.

I reached for some pokeberries and marked my face with jagged lines, then helped Lil Bub lift one end of the raft and walk toward the creek.

When we reached the bank, Bub pulled the wrinkled piece of brown paper from his pocket and spread it on the ground. Down on hands and knees, we formed a tight circle.

My older brother had drawn a skull with crossbones at the top. He had a small building marked "Granary" and tiny trees running north and south beside the creek. Near the huge cottonwood tree southeast of the house was an "XXX" and the word "TREASURE."

I giggled with anticipation. Bub had gone to some trouble to get his plan all put together and it looked like a grand game. I wished immediately for Carolyn who was off in the bend visiting her cousins for the weekend. My best friend did love games on the water.

"All hands on deck," Bub squalled, pointing down the creek. Slowly, we managed to get our raft in the water. It bobbed right along the edge as Bub held tight.

"All aboard," Bub squalled.

I picked up my dog, but when I put one foot on the wobbly raft, Shorty squeezed out of my grasp and jumped free, giving me an "errf" of disapproval.

"Come on, boy, it'll be fun." I crawled onto the raft. Water seeped up between the posts but I was afloat. It was a great feeling, bobbing there above the water. "Come on Shorty, you're gonna miss out."

Clearly, my dog wanted to miss out. He backed up several feet. "Errf, errf, errf," he said, then walked toward the back of the house and plopped down in the deep grass.

"Get aboard, mate," Bub motioned toward Lil Bub.

My younger brother didn't hesitate. He crawled up beside me and the two of us were grinning from ear to ear. "This is somethan, ain't it, Sissy?"

"Move over to the far end, both of you, and stay still. Our weight has to balance out," Bub said.

Soon, the three of us were sitting on the homemade raft, floating grandly down the creek toward the huge cottonwood near the granary.

"Aye," Bub growled at one point. "That would be the South Pacific," he pointed off toward the blackjack trees. "And over there, mates, the corral reefs."

It was about the highest feeling in the world, floating along nice and easy, bare feet dangling off the sides in the cool water, birds singing above, and bullfrogs on the bank watching us pass.

"Land ho," Bub squalled. Getting on his knees, he managed to reach out and grab a willow branch that hung over the creek. He snagged the anchor with both hands and the old raft swung around nicely toward the bank.

Lil Bub and I jumped to the bank and helped pull the raft out of the water while Bub crawled to shore.

"Where's the treasure, Bub?" Lil Bub's eyes were flashing with anticipation.

"Nay," Bub growled, raising his sword. "You will be callin me the Captain, you foolish boy, or it will be your head."

"Captain, which way from here?" I asked.

Bub pulled the map from his pocket, spread it on the ground, and we got in our huddle. "There," he said, putting his finger on the XXX. "The great treasure of the Osage Hills. Why, we must be within a half mile of her." Bub stood, lifted his sword and yelled, "Gold."

The three of us made our way up through the blackjack thicket and around the persimmon trees in a half-circle that led back to the huge cottonwood. We each added color along the way, getting caught up in the imagination of our game.

"Look, over there," I whispered, ducking behind a stump, "Cannibals."

"Let's slaughter em. Leave em in their own blood." My younger brother stood, his stick sword in hand.

The three of us rattled through the trees hitting our sticks against small trees, screaming, falling, wrestling until the battle was won and we stood victorious over our enemy.

On the path that led up to the giant cottonwood, Bub stopped. Pointing down to a fallen log, he knelt on

one knee. "It's one of our own," he said. "An unfortunate soul who musta met his fate seeking the great treasure of the Osage Hills."

All of us paused on our knees in respect. Shorty and
Lil Bub's dog, Shadow, appeared, ambling through the
trees toward us. Shadow was dipping her head shyly,
asking permission to approach.

"Halt," Bub screamed, raising his corn knife high.
"Wild beasts on the path. Man your weapons."

Shorty and Shadow were surprised at the harsh
tone. They stopped and stared. Bub motioned for us to
hurry around and we took off down the hill. Both dogs
came crashing behind, Shorty's shrill "errf, errf" echo-
ing through the brush.

"Halt," Bub squalled, turning back to face the dogs.
He put his big knife right out in front of Shorty, block-
ing his way.

My dog had a puzzled, hurt look on his face. He
wasn't used to being talked to like that. Shadow sat,
threw back her head, and let out a mournful howl that
ended in a kind of yowling talk that made all of us
laugh.

Finally, we were at the cottonwood tree and my
older brother pointed to the spot. Lil Bub and I dived
down on our knees and began to dig in the soft dirt
where Bub had buried something earlier. When I felt
the first thud of metal beneath my hands, I dug faster.

"Gold," Bub yelled above us as we pulled the old
toolbox from the dirt. He plopped to his knees, threw

open the latch on the rusty toolbox and ran his fingers through the smooth rocks inside.

Lil Bub picked up some of the small rocks and stuffed them in his pockets, yelling with pleasure. "Gold, Gold, we've found the treasure of the Osage Hills."

A loud crack of thunder broke the morning calm and we all looked up. The sky that had earlier been sunny and bright was now a weird, chalk yellow and a great mass of black clouds were approaching from the south.

"Quick," Bub said, "Fetch the box and we'll be headin for the ocean. That storm will wreck our ship if we don't get it out to sea."

Lil Bub and I each grabbed a corner of the toolbox and started down the hill toward the creek. But the box was heavy and awkward to carry. We had to stop every few steps and get a better hold.

"Come on with ya," Bub drawled, looking back through his one eye. "What's the hold up there?"

Lil Bub dropped his end of the chest, skinning me from elbow to ankle. "The damned thing is heavy," he cursed. "If you want us to go faster, you come help."

"Mutiny!" Bub cried out, raising his corn knife and taking several steps back to us. "Mess with the Captain and walkin the plank is what you'll be gettin."

Lil Bub twisted his jaw around a time or two and gave Bub a hard look, then he reached down again and took up his end of the rocks.

By the time we reached the bank, Lil Bub and I were out of breath. Bub, fresh as ever, started shouting more orders. "Hoist the anchor. Man the treasure chest.

Let's be off to sea before this storm sends our ship against the rocks."

The wind crashed above us, sending small limbs to the ground and it began to rain. The black cloud was stationed just above and lightning began to pop on the horizon like the cracking of firewood.

"Dad says we should never be around the water when it's stormin," Lil Bub said, casting a worried look at the sky.

"Mutiny again is it?" Bub screamed. He fumbled down in his overalls pockets. My older brother always carried a wide variety of interesting things in his many pockets. On this day, probably for just this occasion, he retrieved a short piece of chain, a padlock, and a key. "A Captain has to protect himself from a mutinous murderer. Fetch your ankle to the treasure box."

Lil Bub took a step backward. "No way, you ain't chainin me to that box of rocks."

"Board up, mate," Bub said, turning to me. "We'll leave this coward for the cannibals."

Lil Bub, apparently resigned to his fate, stepped over and offered his ankle. Bub quickly wrapped the chain snug against Lil Bub's ankle and locked him to the toolbox.

I crawled onto the raft. The rain was coming in a blinding sheet and I had to squint to see Bub's form through the mist. He held fast to the raft. Lil Bub started toward us, struggling with his burden.

"Halt, mate. Prisoners are last to come aboard," Bub said, then he took a long pole limb and stepped onto the raft, holding it in place by digging the stick into the current and putting his weight against it.

A loud crack of thunder shattered above us and lightning streaked through the trees nearby. Lil Bub let out a squall, and with a jump and a roll, he flung himself on the raft. His box hit the corner of the fence posts and the next thing I knew, I was in the creek and a post hit me square in back of the head.

I somehow found the root of a tree and clung there like a roasted marshmallow on a stick. Bub's head bobbed up just beside me. "Oh shit," he said, spitting water, "Oh Shit," he was looking around, frantic to find Lil Bub. "Help me Sissy." All the authority was gone from his voice. "We have to find Lil Bub."

The rain seemed to take on a savage urgency at that moment and the creek was rising by the minute. My heart was pounding in my throat and I could still see interesting little flicks of light in front of my eyes from the post smacking me in the head.

Then Lil Bub's voice screamed out above the storm. "Get me outta here," he howled. I turned my head in the direction of the cry. Through the thick wetness I could barely make out the scene before me.

Lil Bub was in the creek, his ankle held to the bottom by the toolbox of rocks. Luckily, he had somehow landed on a mound of mud so that his head was above the surface. All that was showing was his mouth and nose and eyes and he had his head tilted back and his neck stretched out. He looked like a guppy in a fish bowl, gasping for air.

"I'm comin, Lil Bub. Hold on." Bub dived beneath the surface and bounced back within seconds. "Damn, the box is stuck, I can't budge it."

"Use the key," I screamed.

"It's gone," Bub said, in a hoarse whisper.

Lil Bub could hear none of our conversation because his ears were covered with water. He choked and spit water as the rain continued to pour.

Dad, who had been disking that morning in the far field must have come in when the storm started, gotten worried, and come looking for us. I heard his voice through the rain.

"Sissy, Bub, Lil Bub?"

"Over here," I screamed.

Bub made another quick dive beneath the surface, hoping to dislodge our little brother before Dad saw what was going on. He popped back up just as Dad waded into the creek, bellowing above the storm. "What's wrong?"

Dad reached me. He was up to his shoulders in the rushing creek, struggling to keep his footing. Lifting me from my root, he pushed me safely toward the shore. "Lil Bub. Help Lil Bub," I screamed above the wind.

Within minutes, Dad pulled Lil Bub, toolbox and all to the bank. He collapsed there for a moment, rolling my little brother on his back and pounding his shoulders as Lil Bub choked and gasped for breath.

"Bub, where in hell's the key to this lock?" Dad was looking at us in disbelief, his eyes raging as water dripped from his chin.

"In the creek," Bub yelled back.

"I'll carry Lil Bub, you lift the box of rocks. We have to get out from under these trees."

Dad and Bub stopped at the shop and used the bolt cutters to detach Lil Bub from his box. My younger brother was pale and his teeth were chattering.

"You three get in the house and dry off. Lil Bub, you take a hot shower. I'll be in after I tend to the animals."

It was an eternity before my dad came in. In the meantime, Sis pumped us for details as she fixed supper. "You're dead," she said, adding to our agonizing wait. "Grounded, switched, dead."

When Dad finally came in, he was soaked. He took his sloshing brogan boots off on the porch, grabbed some dry clothes, and walked through the kitchen toward the bathroom. Lil Bub sat, snuggled into a blanket by the woodstove.

"You OK?" Dad asked, looking at Lil Bub.

My little brother nodded.

I was hoping Dad would go ahead and start in on us, get it over with, but he didn't even look at Bub or me. We sat for another excruciating period of time until our father emerged dry and red-faced from the shower.

He made his way slowly to the supper table where we all sat in silence. The bench scraped against the linoleum floor as he wilted onto it. He put his face in his hands for a moment then looked right at Sis.

"You are supposed to be in charge. Did it even occur to you that maybe you should look for them when it started storming and they weren't in the house?"

Sis lifted her right shoulder let it fall, then gave him an innocent look. Excuses didn't work well with my father under these circumstances. Sis was old enough to have learned that much.

Dad's eyes then went to Bub and lingered until I felt my brother squirm beside me on the bench.

"How old are you now?"

"Almost fourteen, sir."

"Humph," Dad grunted with a quick burst of breath. "Fourteen years old and you lock a box of rocks on your little brother's ankle and put him in the creek during a damned storm."

"Yes sir," Bub said, a grim expression on his face. It would do no good to try to explain about the raft or our game. Bub, too, had lived around Dad long enough to know.

My father's eyes settled on me. I looked at him straight on, working my feet together beneath the table. "And you're almost ten. If Bub isn't smart enough to use his head, what about you? If your brother said, 'Sissy, go set fire to the house,' would you do it?"

"No sir," I said.

Dad let out a deep sigh. "If any one of you lives to be twenty-one, I'll feel a great sense of accomplishment."

"Yes sir," we all said in unison.

"You two," he said, pointing at Bub and me. "You two are grounded for a month. I have gates that need painting. There's limbs to pick up, yard work. I'll make you a list."

"Yes sir," Bub and I agreed.

"No company at all during this month."

"No sir."

"And ..." he said, then let the silence hang in the air.

I held my breath waiting for the announcement of the peach tree switch that was coming.

"I'd switch the hide off of you both," he gave another sigh and reached for the pot of beans in front of him, "But I'm just too damned tired to do it."

X

Bub and I remained grounded up until the day of our annual school picnic. The evening before, my brother tried to have a discussion with me about the possibility of our being able to attend.

"I reckon Dad won't let us go to the picnic at Braden tomorrow." Bub said, as we finished our barn chores.

Trying to ignore him, I busied myself gathering eggs. I hadn't spoken to him since the day of the pirate game. Bub was trouble and I'd had enough of his foolish notions that always got me strapped with extra chores and peach tree switchings.

My brother had attempted conversation with me many times the past weeks and I knew my silence was beginning to irritate him.

"Wonder if there isn't some way we could get in Dad's good graces?" he asked, coming over next to me and slumping onto a bale of hay. His face suddenly sparked with an idea. "I've got it! We could volunteer to

117

do all the work tomorrow for the picnic. Save Dad the trouble. We can kill the chicken, fry it, make potato salad and baked beans, all that stuff Dad usually helps Sis with."

I nonchalantly placed the last egg in my basket and started out of the barn.

Bub followed right behind me as my bare feet puffed along the path toward the house. "Yep, bet that will work. If we allow him to have the day off while we get everything ready, how can he make us stay home?"

I paused in the creek, letting the cool water travel lovingly up around my ankles. For a moment I imagined Carolyn and me at the bridge, embarking on an adventure in the wonderful warm sunshine. May, my favorite month, was nearly gone and I hadn't played with my friend one time except at school.

"Don't you think that's a grand idea, Sissy?" Bub asked, stepping right in front of me.

I glared at him, my squinted eyes burning with all the hatred I could muster. With one hand, I pushed him aside and continued on my way.

That evening at the supper table, Bub revealed his wonderful plan.

"Sissy and I want to do all the food for the picnic tomorrow," he said, with a dashing little smile. "We've agreed on it, haven't we Sissy?" He cast a quick look at me, nodded "yes" for me, then continued. "We'll save you and Sis the bother and it will give us some good experience."

Dad's expression was passive at first as he tore into his roast sandwich, but after a few moments I could see he was giving the notion serious consideration.

"Actually, that might just work out. Sis and I need to go in for groceries tomorrow because I'll be busy on Saturday. We'll take Lil Bub, so you and Sissy can tie right in and ... and if you do a good job, you can go to the picnic tomorrow afternoon."

It always amazed me how Bub could figure things out with Dad. His talent for maneuvering events sometimes exceeded his knack for creating havoc.

"When you two finish in the kitchen in the morning," Dad said, "You can gather up some gunnysacks for the races tomorrow and fetch you a terrapin apiece."

Those words did bring a spark of life back to me. Not only were we going to the picnic, we'd be able to take part in the competitions as well.

The next morning when the old pickup rattled off down the gravel road, my brother was in the highest of spirits. Strangely, Bub loved being in the kitchen. Cooking held a great fascination for him and although he rarely had the time, when he was unleashed at the stove, he seemed to savor the opportunity.

"Look at these, Sissy," he had several recipe cards lined up on the counter, examining them. "Did you know what all goes into a nice potato salad? Celery, cucumber, garlic, paprika, two kinds of pickles. Wow. Interesting. And look at the baked beans: green onions, brown sugar, Worcestershire sauce. Fascinating."

I knew he was doing his best to make me utter a word, but my mind was made up. I would never talk to Bub again as long as I lived. I shifted my weight from one foot to the other, waiting for him to assign me a task.

"Let's see, there's hard-boiled eggs to peel, potatoes to wash, beans to fix, or ... you can go kill the chicken. If you've got the nerve?"

I knew he added the last dig because he wanted me to do it. He wanted to stay in the kitchen while I did the nasty duty of cutting the head from a pullet and picking the sticky feathers. But, in a way, I wanted to show him. He thought he was so smart. I could kill a chicken. I'd seen Mama do it plenty of times. And besides, he could have the hot kitchen. I'd rather be outside for awhile in the nice spring air.

Without replying, I turned and tramped out, letting the screen door bang when I walked outside. Stomping out to the chicken house, I cornered a young pullet. Carrying the chicken by the rubbery feet, I marched toward the chopping block and the axe.

If I did it quick, I'd show Bub. It came to me, as I heisted up the heavy axe and got a good hold on the chicken, that I hadn't ever killed anything. My brothers both tormented the wild birds with their BB guns and accosted the squirrels and rabbits with 22 rifles, but I ignored their savagery.

For a long time, I'd had a struggle with certain things regarding our farm existence. Befriending every animal on the place, I sometimes violently protested the slaughter of my beloved critters for food. It was, however, something my father refused to even discuss, and after several harsh confrontations that ended in the peach tree switch, I learned to conform.

Thinking about it was only going to make it worse. After all, I loved fried chicken as well as the next person. I drew the old axe up and "slap" it came down hard and fast and right on target. The pullet's head went flying off of the board and its body started jumping and trembling in my hand. I flung the burden away from me, horrified, and watched as it flopped and twisted leaving a trail of blood.

Turning away, I looked down at the chopping block and stared in shock at the head, lying sticky with its eyes glaring.

All at once my belly went sour and I leaned over on the nearby peach tree and puked. Sweat beads bubbled up on my forehead and I clung to the tree, my legs shaking. Finally, I straightened, wiped my face with the back of my sleeve, and tried to regain my composure.

I heard the kitchen window squeak open and saw Bub's face shining behind the screen. "What's wrong, did it get sick?" He asked, in a soft, caring voice.

A streak of anger vibrated through me like a rumbling freight train. I stared down at the cold body and knew I had to pick it up, but I couldn't bring my feet to move.

"Well," Bub shouted from the kitchen window, "does it want Bubby to come pick it up?"

That did it, I took two quick steps, grabbed the dead chicken by its feet and started for the house.

My brother, once he knew he had someone going, had little resistance to silence. "Poor little Sissy, a tender heart, can't kill a flea, can you gal?" He poured hot water over the chicken in the sink as I stood, trying to quiet the seething that steamed within me toward my older brother.

I began plucking feathers as fast as I could, trying to take my anger out on the pullet and ignore my irritating brother.

Bub stood at the stove, chunking hot potatoes from the pan into a large mixing bowl. "Poor little Sissy," he continued. After a short silence, he let out a choke of laughter. "Poor little Sissy, she went to kill a chick. What she didn't know was that it would make her sick." He sung out the words in a fine tune then bent over and slapped his leg, howling.

I plucked faster, feeling the color rise in my neck.

"Come on, lighten up, Sissy. You take life way to serious." He fetched a wet smelly feather from the sink in front of me and ran it up along the back of my neck. "Tickle, tickle, tickle."

It was an instant reaction. A reflex I had no control over. I drew back my pullet and "splat" I slapped my brother across the face. The blow was so hard, it knocked Bub backward into the stove sending a clatter of potatoes and boiled eggs spiraling across the linoleum floor behind him.

When my older brother looked up, he had blood and wet feathers smeared across his face and a sharp look of vengeance in his eyes. I dived into the nearest retreat, the bathroom. Slamming the door, I slid the lock in place just before Bub crashed against the wood with all his weight. He threw himself into his task, jarring the old door against its lock, but to my relief the screws held.

In the long silence that followed, I hated my decision to trap myself in the bathroom. If I'd run outside, my brother only had half a chance to catch me. I was a fast runner and had a thousand places to hide. But I had incarcerated myself for the afternoon in the close quarters of the bathroom where Bub could terrorize me.

My brother's face soon appeared outside the bathroom window. He'd pulled a sawhorse up and was glaring down at me like a spider at a fly. "I'm gonna get you, Sissy and you're gonna eat that half-plucked chicken." He began to fiddle with some tools against the window.

I grabbed the door handle, with a quick jerk I unlocked the door and was going to run outside to freedom. The door wouldn't budge. Bub's laughter echoed against the window glass.

"You're trapped, Sister dear. I put a chair outside the door. You're mine."

A streaking fear went through me. My mind raced to come up with another option.

"Darn," Bub said, "Gotta have some more tools. Don't go anywhere Sissy." Bub giggled as he jumped from the sawhorse. I watched on tiptoes as he disappeared around the corner of the house.

My eyes searched the perimeter of the bathroom and settled on the small opening above the shower that went into the attic. By simply pushing the trapdoor up, a person could crawl into the attic and travel across the ceiling of the living room to the far side of the house where there was another opening that led outside.

I hesitated, staring upward. I'd only peeked into the blackness of the hole once when Dad was working there. It was an ominous place that held electric wires and other unknown obstacles. Could I possibly make it through? Sometimes on winter nights I heard soft, scuffling noises in the attic and Bub said it was rats. I suddenly wished for my dog.

Jumping up on the dirty-clothes hamper and stretching my hands to the top of the metal edge of the shower, I pulled myself up, pushed the door open, and squeezed in, letting the small door fall back in place.

I chuckled in the darkness and was immediately glad of my decision. What a good joke on Bub. He'd work for the better part of an hour getting the window off, then find me gone.

Surmising the situation in the total darkness, some of my gaiety faded. The attic was forbidden to us kids for several reasons. I remembered Dad saying something about having to stay on the rafters or a person could put a foot right through the ceiling of the house. And I knew nothing about the wiring, but held visions of touching something that would fry me like a potato in hot oil.

My eyes tried to adjust to the absence of light. It was the blackest kind of black and I knew I was going to have to feel my way along the precarious journey. I took a couple of deep breaths. Dad liked to say, "*A journey begins with a single step.*"

Making my way inch by inch on my hands and knees, I scooted along in total darkness, spurred by the thought that Bub was working futilely at the bathroom window below.

Then, I thought I heard something. I stopped, quieting my breath, listening. What if I met up with a big rat while I was trying to balance on those thin rafters? For a moment, I considered backing up, but that would be nearly impossible. Twice my feet had scraped against the Sheetrock and I cringed, knowing Dad would spot the slightest crack in the ceiling.

I lowered my head and started off again. My heart hammered when I caught the first hint of light coming through the crack around the opening at the far end of the house. With fresh determination, I dipped my head and proceeded.

Then I heard something for sure. I stopped and listened. It was a muffled sort of scraping that seemed to stop when I stopped. All of a sudden, I wanted out of the attic in the worst way. Visions of vampires and bats leaped through my mind, stinging me with fear. Head back down, I was scrambling toward the dim light in the distance when I slammed against a solid obstacle.

Something reached out and grabbed me. I reared up in an attempt to fight, hit my head on a maze of wires and fell, breaking, crashing, screaming through the ceiling.

The thing had hold of me and I was fighting to get untangled. I heard a squeak and moan and the old couch in the front room split at the seams, heaved one last breath, and fell in two pieces.

"Oh shit, oh dear," I heard my brother's voice and blinked my eyes in disbelief. Bub and I were tangled in a lump between the flattened couch and broken Sheetrock. I still had one hand gripped to his overalls strap and he was clinging to my foot. We sat for a moment, staring at the gaping hole in the ceiling.

It was obvious then, what I'd heard and what I'd hit. When my brother had gone to fetch his tools, he'd spotted the opening outside at the opposite end of the house that led to the attic and conceived the idea of surprising me. I could picture him stretching the extension ladder up from the outside, whistling with amusement, then proceeding along his merry way.

The noise I'd heard was him. He'd heard me. We'd stopped at the exact same times when we'd heard each other, then had both proceeded at breakneck speed toward our destinations, crashing head on.

"Why in the hell did you get up in the attic?" Bub said, "You know the attic is off-limits."

I wanted to kill him. Just murder him and hide his bones. I glared, but couldn't come up with anything mean enough to say. I rubbed the top of my head where it throbbed and stared at the huge hole in the ceiling. There wasn't any way of hiding it or covering it up.

"Well," Bub said, standing and beginning to pick up the broken pieces of ceiling. "It's done. We better clean up the mess at least, and get the food ready. If we're lucky we may live another day." He grinned. "But maybe not."

I hated him. His curious sense of detachment when he'd once again put my life on the line. I knew Dad would switch us until he peeled hide, any plans for the picnic were history, and probably I'd be grounded for the entire summer.

But, I also knew he was right. Our options were limited. If we cleaned up the mess and had the food prepared when Dad returned from town, it might somehow soften the blow.

My father came into the house with two armloads of brown grocery bags. He somehow missed the ceiling on the way into the kitchen. Great bowls of potato salad, cole slaw, and baked beans sent wonderful aromas through the house. Golden fried chicken sat brown and crispy on a glass platter.

"Umm," Dad said, setting his bags on the counter. Sticking a finger in the potato salad, then the beans, he got a look of pleasure on his face. "Bub, you're gonna make somebody a good wife one of these days."

My brother chuckled at the joke. I stared at him, disbelieving. He knew we were about to get whipped and he was laughing.

"You two all ready to go to the picnic?" Dad turned, jerking up a crunchy piece of gizzard from the chicken plate. He walked to the icebox, poured himself a mug of iced tea then started for the front room, talking the whole while. "It's a great day for the picnic. I'll bet everyone in Osage County comes out. Ice cream, soda pop, games ..." He plopped down on the couch and I closed my eyes.

Bub had put some effort into repairing the worn couch by hammering several large nails in strategic places, but when Dad's weight hit the piece of furniture, it gave a slow wheeze, moaned, and ripped back into pieces.

Dad's iced tea went spiraling up, splashing back into his face, and he landed flat on his back, looking up. His eyes traveled straight to the startling new development in the ceiling.

"What in the name of ..." He scrambled up, iced tea dripping from his chin, took three giant steps toward us and grabbed Bub and me by the ears.

"I don't even want to know," he said, as he ushered us toward the back porch and out the old screen door. "No. I don't care. Both of you walk yourselves out and pick a switch from the peach tree. I'll be out directly."

When Bub and I turned to start outside, Dad said, "If you have any problems picking a choice switch, I'll help."

Both of us knew what that meant. On occasion, knowing we were about to be thrashed with a limb, we'd find a flimsy wimp of a switch that broke easily after two stings.

Beneath the peach trees, I stood and stared up, letting out a sigh.

"Decisions, decisions," Bub said, real cheerful.

I looked at him with a dagger glance. He'd cost me most of my carefree playing time in the spring with Carolyn, now I'd miss the competitions at the school picnic and God only knew what was ahead.

I spotted the bloody axe that was leaning against the chopping block. "I'll pick yours," I said. I lifted the axe and pushed it toward him, handle first.

He stood for a moment with a perplexed look on his face, then his head bounced back and his laughter rolled out over the hills. The sound of it brought the flicker of a smile to my lips.

XI

By the fall of 1958, Mama and Dad's divorce was final and my mother had remarried. That September an atmosphere of doom hovered over our lives.

Dad worked from daylight until dark, red-stubble beard and dust on his face, exhaustion in his eyes. He took little interest in anything other than our basic needs. When Sis began to talk about things she "had" to have for her senior year of high school, Dad gave her a weary look across the table. "You have what you have," he growled, which sent my sister crying to her bedroom.

All of us walked a wide circle around our father during those first few months after the divorce because he was long on anger and short on patience. If he wasn't farming or working his railroad job, he was drinking home brew.

One bright Saturday in late October, when the leaves were twisting in the breeze with golden lights, we loaded up to go into Ponca City for groceries. Dad's dark humor had infected us all with a case of brooding silence.

"Let's play Barnyard Poker," Bub said to me and Lil Bub as we settled into the bed of the old pickup.

The idea of a game immediately sparked my spirit. I sat up and agreed with a nod just as Dad pulled the truck off the gravel and onto the paved road heading west.

Lil Bub and I would team up against Bub. We chose the south side of the road and Bub took the north. Cows and horses counted one point, sheep and hogs five, and white horses twenty. You could only count the animals as you passed. If there was a huge herd, it wasn't fair to just shout, "Fifty." You had to say, "one-two-three-four-five" until you could no longer see to count.

The object was to have the highest points by the time we reached the Arkansas River bridge on the outskirts of town.

The fine autumn day made the game especially appealing, as we sat in the bed of the truck, breathing the crisp air and looking through the maze of golden-red trees.

Lil Bub and I worked diligently on our side, racking up over a hundred by the time we passed Colby's ranch. Bub was barely trailing us, bouncing and shouting and pointing as animals appeared and disappeared along the highway.

Just as we approached the bridge, my older brother shouted, "Twenty, forty, sixty, eighty. Wow, four white horses there, behind that stand of blackjacks."

"Cheat," Lil Bub squealed, squinting in the direction of the trees.

"I won," Bub smirked from his perch on the spare tire. "Two hundred points. You two owe me a stick of penny candy each."

"Bub, you are so full of it. There aren't four white horses in all of Osage County." I said, shaking my head.

"Are you callin me a liar?" My brother got a serious look on his face.

"Yes, I guess I am. A liar. A cheat. A pain in the butt."

Bub's face cracked back into a grin. "You're a poor sport, Sissy."

"And you ... are exasperating." I snarled at him. "We were havin a real decent game. Why do you always mess things up?"

Lil Bub, who was just learning to count, had worked hard for nine miles. He reached and gave Bub a little shove.

The fight was on, the three of us attached to each other in this bumping, swatting lump, moving in the bed of the pickup like a spinning top.

The brakes suddenly slammed which threw us toward the cab. My father's thick fingers thumped across the back glass and we immediately took our places, sitting with hands in our lap. It was a first warning. If Dad touched the brakes a second time, he'd have the pickup pulled alongside of the highway and we would be in big trouble.

By the time we reached Ponca City, all of us were waiting for a second chance to have a go at each other. Dad and Sis emerged from the pickup and walked into the grocery store.

"Cheater," Lil Bub said, sneering at Bub.

"Baby boy," Bub said, prodding Lil Bub with his index finger.

"Leave him be," I said. "You started it, Bub."

About that time three teenage boys appeared on the sidewalk and hesitated, their heads together, casting little glances over toward us and whispering.

"Howdy," I said, giving them a grin.

They broke into laughter, looking at each other as they pointed and slapped their legs. They were wearing white T-shirts, black leather jackets, and jeans that hung low on their hips. They each had sideburns and long hair slicked back with oil. I guessed them to be close to Bub in age.

"Hoowwdy," one of the boys drawled to the other.

The friendly smile faded from my face, and when Bub stood up and jumped over onto the sidewalk, I followed.

"What part of the sticks did you three crawl out of?" one of the other boys asked.

"We're Osage County Kids," Lil Bub bragged, standing in the back of the truck and tucking his fingers under the straps of his overalls.

That really sent the three into a fit. One of them mocked my younger brother's words, putting his fingers up on his chest.

"Look at that girl," one of them said. "Barefooted with overalls." They all went into a hooting scream of laughter.

With a sinking sense of shame, I stared at the three. They weren't just teasing and making fun the way we did with each other. The boys were laughing at us. At who we were. I felt embarrassed at first, then mad.

Bub dived into them, jabbing one boy right in the gut with his fist. He jumped and squalled, knocking two of them down, and I took the third when he recovered from his belly punch. I grabbed my boy from behind, getting a death grip on his neck. He spun around and around, choking out little gurgling noises.

My brother knew how to fight. He and Sis had a go at it often enough, popping each other with fists and wrestling, but since Bub had gone into town school, he'd gained a reputation for being a "scrapper."

Out of the corner of my eye, I saw Lil Bub come to my aid. He grabbed my boy around the legs, sinking a tooth into an exposed ankle. The gurgling turned into a scream, the boy toppled forward, and Lil Bub and I grabbed his arms and twisted them up behind him.

Bub, who at first had his hands full, was doing a fine job of handling the other two, when I heard my father yell.

When I turned, the boy we had pinned quickly struggled free and I felt a hard "blap" right across my nose. The pain was instant and sharp. I bent and a gush of warm blood oozed as I put my hand to my face.

"Get in the truck," Dad's voice bellowed out over the quiet street. Several onlookers across at the feed store stopped to stare as my older brother continued to whack the offenders.

Dad gave Lil Bub and me a quick shove, stepped through the maze and caught Bub by the shirt collar. When he first pulled my brother back, I thought Bub would hit Dad. His eyes were glazed and the veins in his neck were extended, and he didn't recognize Dad at first.

"Lad, settle down, settle down now," Dad said, holding my brother at arm's-length. "What in the hell's going on out here, anyway?"

The three boys slowly stood, gathering themselves. They had blood-splattered faces and disheveled hair and one of them had a fine shiner already appearing around his right eye. They took a look at my father and started off, limping and cursing.

Bub's face was white and splotched with red, his shirt was torn completely off of his arms, hanging by the collar where Dad held him. His lip was bloody, but he had an expression of pure satisfaction on his face.

"What happened out here?" Dad asked again.

Bub wallowed his tongue around, licking the blood from his lip, and spit. "They was makin fun of Sissy and Lil Bub."

Dad didn't react the way I expected. Usually for fighting, we'd end up with a serious scolding and sometimes the switch. This was different in Dad's mind, I could tell. In fact, he almost seemed proud of Bub.

"That lip OK?" Dad asked, pulling Bub's chin up.

"Yes sir."

"Well, I'd say they got the worst end of the deal." Then he turned and handed me his handkerchief, examining my nose. He started back for the grocery store, without another word.

My older brother flexed his shoulders and kind of shook his upper body, like a dog getting up from a nap. We were all still talking about the fight when Dad came out and began to set boxes of groceries around us in the bed of the pickup.

Instead of Dad pulling the old truck out and heading east toward the farm, he turned and went south. When he walked into the Santa Fe railroad station I didn't think too much about it at first. Sometimes he stopped to get his check or talk to his boss. But when I heard the distant whistle and realized the passenger train was rumbling in, I felt a flush of excitement. All of us looked at each other expectantly.

A few minutes later, Dad emerged carrying a big suitcase and our Grandma Carrie was walking right beside him. All of us let out a whoop and dived over the side and out of the cab to greet Grandma.

"We're kind of beat up, Mother. But still here," Dad said, apologetically, looking at my bloody nose and Bub's ripped shirt.

"Look at that wonderful red hair," Grandma said to Lil Bub.

"Those brilliant blue eyes," she said, looking at me.

"Bub, you've grown three inches," she admired Bub's muscled arms beneath the torn shirt.

"And look here," Grandmother said, taking Sis by the hand. "A young lady. The boys will be callin now."

My Grandmother's presence touched us like a magic wand. As we took her suitcase and she crawled into the cab, a fresh spirit bubbled up inside me. Things at the farm would be different now.

Grandma fixed a pot roast with new potatoes and green beans that first evening for supper. She baked buttermilk biscuits that melted in my mouth and served each of us a generous slice of crispy apple pie.

"So my daddy, your great grandfather, sent me out to the garden to pick a bucket of string beans." Grandma's stories held me spellbound. "It was a beautiful spring day in Arkansas, the creek was swollen from the rains, birds singing. I wanted to play, not work in the garden. So, I picked about a half bucket, and just fooling around, I reached into my bucket and fluffed those beans up with my fingers real lightly. Well, to my surprise, they expanded into a full bucket. I marched back to the house and before I walked in, I fluffed up those beans, then presented them to Daddy."

"What happened, Grandma?" The four of us asked at once.

"He took my bucket and looked at me over the top of his glasses, then he whacked that bucket three or four times hard against the floor. Both of us watched as the full bucket settled quickly into a half."

Everyone laughed. Even Dad gave a soft chuckle as he swished his iced tea around in its mug. "Don't give them any ideas, Mother. They have plenty of their own."

"What did your daddy do?" Sis asked.

"He made me memorize five Bible verses and pick two full buckets of beans."

"What was it like growin up in Arkansas, Grandma?" I tried to picture a place different from Oklahoma.

Grandma thought dreamily for a few moments before she answered. "Water so clear you can see to the bottom of the deepest rivers. Many, many trees of every sort. Gooseberries, strawberries, blackberries, grow wild. The seasons are flush with color and freshness of every sort," she said, fondly.

I thought for a moment of my strict, straight-lipped father growing up. What had he been like then? Did grandmother switch him and was he always in trouble the way us kids seemed to be?

"How did you meet grandfather?" Sis asked, turning and scooting closer so she wouldn't miss one word.

"Phillip Mathias Jacobs," Grandma said, then grinned. "Well, I hate to disappoint you, Sis, but it wasn't very romantic."

"Tell us, Grandma," the four of us chimed.

"I was nearly eighteen years old. My little brothers had talked me into helping them catch tadpoles from the pond. That's the first time I saw him. He came riding up on the family mule and we started visiting."

"Where did you go on a date?" Sis wanted more.

"To church. Back then church was the center of our social life. We had box suppers, dances, socials. It was the only place for two young people to court."

Having Grandma Carrie on the farm filled us all with new life. She spent her mornings teaching Sis and me little tricks about baking, laundry, and sewing. In the afternoons, she took special time with each of us just talking and listening.

Every evening, she insisted we all bathe, wash our hair, brush our teeth, then gather around while she read from her fat Bible. Sometimes the Bible readings bored me and all of us became restless, twitching about and picking at one another. But after a few days, the routine of it was kind of nice and I even began to look forward to the quiet togetherness before bedtime.

Grandma went with Bub to look at his pigs, see his F.F.A. sign up at the cattle guard, and listen to his dreams of the Air Force. She followed Lil Bub on a relentless journey to capture bugs and to my astonishment, even allowed Herman the tarantula to crawl up around her shoulders onto her head. Sis and Grandma spent a lot of time in the back bedroom, fitting patterns, playing with hair styles and talking "Girl Talk."

One afternoon Grandma joined Carolyn and me at the bridge for a picnic. She took off her high-laced shoes, heisted up her long dress and waded with us, then sat at our stump table for peanut butter and jelly sandwiches.

"You two girls have a great place to play," she said, admiring our hideout with her eyes. "And isn't it grand that you each have a special dog?" Shorty and Fly Boy sat nearby, waiting for a scrap from our table.

"Maybe Carolyn could ride with me next summer on the train to visit you," I said, the idea filling me with joy.

Grandma giggled. "Wouldn't that be fun? The three of us could go to church together, visit the neighbors, go shopping. You two could make a playhouse in the attic."

Carolyn's eyes got big and we both let out a whoop of excitement. "I didn't know you had an attic, Grandma."

She leaned toward us and whispered, "I've been saving it for just the right occasion."

"Maybe Fly Boy and Shorty could come with us on the train?" I yelped out the wonderful idea.

Grandma let out a hearty roll of laughter. "It's a great idea, Sissy, but I don't think the train conductor allows dogs."

The two weeks Grandma spent with us turned all of our lives around. A new sense of order began to take shape and Dad's interaction with us kids softened. So when the announcement came one morning that our grandmother would be leaving the next day on the morning train, my spirits took a dive.

Grandma must have seen the disappointment in our faces that morning, so she came up with an idea to keep us kids busy. "You know, I've got a hunger for catfish. Why don't you three go down to the pond this afternoon and catch us a mess of nice fish for supper."

"Sure, Grandma, as soon as I finish up morning chores." Bub answered, because Grandma was looking at him. "Why, we'll bring you back the best stringer of catfish you've seen since you left Arkansas."

"OK, then," Grandma said. "Sis and I have a dress to finish and some laundry to get done. You three catch the fish and we'll cook them."

That afternoon as we trudged toward the pond, Lil Bub and I were grumbling. "I don't see why she has to go," my younger brother said, pouting.

"Why can't she just sell her house in Purcell and move in with us on the farm?" I said.

"Because she has her own life, that's why," Bub explained. "She'll be back."

Lil Bub and I were still rigging up our cane poles and baiting our hooks when Bub plopped his line in the water. He hadn't even settled himself on the bank when his cork began to dance sending ripples out across the still pond.

"Oh boy," Bub said, standing. Lil Bub and I both looked just in time to see that ole catfish run with the line. Then "plunk" the cork disappeared and my brother let out a yelp and began to pull.

For the next hour, we hauled in two nice catfish apiece. The joy of catching fish had brought back my spirit. Bub challenged me to walk the pipelines with him, so we left Lil Bub fishing and started off on the far side of the dam.

Twelve-inch pipes crossed up in a rainbow spiral four or five feet from the ground. Bub started off like a high-wire artist at a circus, holding his hands to his sides for balance. I followed, trying to copy my brother's speed and agility.

Just as we began playing, a cottontail rabbit lumbered out of the oak brush, hopped along just beneath us, then disappeared quickly into the drainpipe that went through the pond dam.

Bub let out a whoop. "Wonder when Grandma had rabbit last? If she likes catfish, she'd love a plump rabbit to fry up. Come on, Sissy, help me just a minute."

My brother gathered up some leaves and pulled a box of matches from his overalls.

"Dad will switch you for usin those matches," I said. It hadn't been a week since Dad lectured us about how dry it was and not to be playing with fire.

"He'll never know," Bub said, whispering. He stuffed the leaves into the drainpipe, added a few twigs, and struck a match. Soon, a trickle of smoke began to spiral up into the autumn wind. "Hurry Sissy," Bub screamed, running up over the dam to the other end of the pipe.

He grabbed two tree limbs and handed me one as we stationed ourselves at the end of the pipe near the dam. "I'll stand right here," Bub said, putting himself closest to the pipe. "You stand behind me a few feet. Just in case I miss him, you get him."

I knew I wouldn't have the heart to club the rabbit, but I was sucked right into my brother's excitement, so I played along.

Smoke began to trickle out of our end of the pipe. Bub picked up his feet and hopped around in a circle. "We're bringin home a rabbit, Grandma, won't you be surprised. A rabbit and a stringer of catfish. We're hunters and gatherers, we're happy and smart."

I was grinning at my older brother's antics and began to dance along, swinging my stick above my head. Lil Bub appeared at the top of the dam.

"I got another one. Whatcha doin?"

"We're huntin rabbits," Bub yelled. "Keep catchin fish, little brother."

Lil Bub waved and disappeared back over the dam just as something made a scratching sound from the pipe. "Get ready, Sissy," Bub whispered, pulling back his stick.

Shorty and Shadow ran around our feet, eager to help with our hunt. Shorty let out an "errf" of excitement.

Two eyes appeared, barely visible in the darkness of the drainpipe. When the face broke into the light, it wasn't a rabbit, but the pointed nose of a skunk. Bub had his stick started in a swing before he realized what he was about to hit. He let the stick go spinning into midair. The skunk came shuffling out of that drainpipe fairly unconcerned. Unfortunately for us all, both dogs dived right into the poor skunk.

"Run, Sissy, Run," Bub squalled, and the two of us took off as fast as we could. It was too late, though. Just as my bare feet got traction and I started to move, that skunk let his weapon fly. The wind was coming toward us and the juice came with it.

I kept on moving as fast as my feet would scramble, but within seconds I was blind and my nose was burning with the stench. I tried to suck air through my mouth and felt like I'd swallowed fourteen grasshoppers and they were all wanting out. I fell down against a tree trunk and commenced clawing and grasping for help of any kind.

"Jeeessus Chrrristt!" I heard Bub choke.

I began to roll and rub myself in the grass like I'd seen my dog do when he'd met up with a skunk. I rolled over and over, sliding through the grass blindly, like a snake shot through the head.

Finally, I lay exhausted. Tears were running out of my blind eyes, and slobber was drooling from my gaping mouth as I sucked the wind for one nibble of oxygen, like a fish out of water. I sat up and whimpered just as my dog dived into my lap. The intensity of my smell was nothing compared to Shorty's. The solid slam of fresh skunk put me mercifully to sleep. I crashed backward into the thick brush.

"Sissy, Sissy wake up," Bub was shaking my shoulder, standing over me. "We have to get to the house and try to get some of this off." He sneezed and wheezed, then spit. "Lil Bub took the fish and left. He couldn't stand the smell."

I sat up and took a rattling breath that made me choke. I rubbed my scratchy eyes, coughed, and let out a moan. "Oh Bub, I hurt in so many places ..." I began to bawl with great howls of grief.

"It's terrible bad, that's a fact. Get up, Sissy, come on, we'll go wash some of it off." Bub hauled me to my feet and led me down the path toward home.

Dad came out the door with a bang, walking toward us as we entered the yard. "This is a fine stunt for you two to pull right before your grandmother leaves." He took three angry strides toward us then stopped dead still, staring.

"Good God," he bellowed, stepping back. "You two aren't hardly worth the effort it'll take to clean you up."

"No sir," we agreed.

Grandma stepped out of the house with two gallon jars of tomato juice, one under each arm. "Fetch a couple of washtubs, Dean. Let's soak these little stinkers."

My dad didn't share any of Grandma's enthusiasm, but he walked off toward the shop, shaking his head.

"Oh, Lah," Grandma said, stepping toward us. She let out a fine chuckle. "So you were going to catch me a rabbit to go along with the catfish, I hear. Well, Lil Bub brought back a fine stringer of fish, so we'll do just fine for supper."

Even the mention of food made my sick stomach roll. I let go of Bub who'd been half carrying me and sank to the ground. On hands and knees I began to gasp and puke.

Grandma walked right over to me and held my head with her soft hands. I don't know how she stood the stench, but she stayed right with me until Dad showed up with the tubs.

At sundown Bub and I continued to soak in our tubs of tomato juice in the yard. Shorty shared my tub. When I invited him to join me in the thick, red juice, my dog bolted. Lil Bub and Sis cornered him finally and brought him wiggling over to me. I held him captive, rinsing him from head to foot. The two of us shivered in the chill of the autumn evening as the sun disappeared into a mess of bright orange clouds.

Grandma brought a wonderful plate of fried catfish, poke greens, and hush puppies to Bub and me. The food smelled wonderful, but when I took a bite of the crispy fish, it tasted just like skunk, so I quietly fed the food to my dog one bite at a time.

From the open kitchen window the clatter of plates and forks rattled out into the yard as everyone but Bub and me finished up the last supper with Grandma. When I heard Sis running water into the sink to wash dishes, Grandma appeared with shampoo and towels.

She scrubbed me from head to toe, then wrapped me warmly in a towel. "You dash in there and take a shower now. Wash yourself again, then rinse your hair and body with vinegar. I left a jug of it in the shower. And hurry, Bub will be right behind you."

"Yes ma'm."

When Bub and I emerged from our showers, soaked, scrubbed, and rinsed, the smell was still on us. As I slipped into fresh clothes, I heard Dad talking to Grandma from the living room.

"They can't sleep in their beds, they'll ruin the sheets, mattress and all. I guess they can each take an old blanket and have a pallet outside. Sissy sleeps out near the creek half the time anyway. And school tomorrow. I'll have to talk to Mrs. B. Maybe she can move their desks out onto the porch for a week or so."

"This too shall pass, son," Grandma said, in a comforting tone.

"I oughta take the switch to them," Dad said, his voice angry.

"Nonsense," Grandma said, "Don't you think they've been through enough. They're just ..." Grandma searched for the exact word. "... Inventive. That's all."

"Ummm." My Dad groaned. "You should have them every day. You'd think inventive."

"I had you, didn't I?" Grandma's voice held amusement. "And Bill, Eunice, Rhea, and Alma. One of these days you'll look back and laugh at these times."

That last evening on the farm, Grandma read to us from the book of Job. She had Sis and Lil Bub and Dad sit outside at the picnic table with her while Bub and I listened nearby from our place on the ground.

I listened intently as Grandma's voice traveled softly through the darkness. I watched the lightning bugs flashing out in the fields and the June bugs and millers banging against the porch light.

"There was a man in the land of Uz, whose name was Job; and that man was perfect and upright, and one that feared God, and eschewed evil ... The fire of God is fallen from heaven, and hath burned up the sheep ... and fell upon the camels, and have carried them away, yea and slain the servants with the edge of the sword ... and behold there came a great wind from the wilderness, and smote the four corners of the house, and it fell upon the young men and they are dead ... and smote Job with sore boils from the sole of his foot unto his crown."

Something about the story began to connect with my summer experiences. In between grandmother's words, my mind carried me back to the incident of the dugout, the pirate game, the attic. My beautiful spring and summer days being turned into extra chores and peach tree switchings. Now it was autumn and I couldn't even enjoy the brisk air because I smelled like a skunk. I swallowed, and the dead taste in my mouth made me think of the morning. Bub had turned a peaceful day of fishing into a fiasco.

When Grandma stopped reading, the sound of tree frogs chorused from the creek and a coyote howled from a distant hill.

"Did Job have a big brother?" I asked, from the darkness, breaking the silence.

Bub laughed first. He fell backwards into his quilt, holding his sides, choking out rolling howls. Grandma joined in and soon the yard was filled with the wonderful music of laughter.

Epilogue

That night in September, 1958, Bub and I sat outside on our quilts and talked long after the lights went out in the house.

"I don't want Grandma to go home tomorrow," I said, looking up at the stars and cuddling my dog.

"Things change, Sissy, like I've told you. You have to roll with the punches."

"Bub," I said, watching a firefly blink across the creek. "Grandma's gettin old, isn't she?"

"I reckon."

"She'll die sometime."

"Yeah, sometime."

"What do you suppose happens to us when we die?"

"It's a great mystery, Sissy. Tell you what, I'll die first, then I'll come back and tell you all about it." Bub chuckled in the darkness.

"No," I snapped.

"No?"

"Bub, I don't want you to die first. I'd be lonesome without you."

Bub's laughter echoed out across the creek and tickled back into my ears. "There's a lot of things you don't want, isn't there, Sissy? Well, I'm older than you, so I reckon I'll go first. But ... tell you what I'll do. I'll make sure you know I'm OK."

I jumped up on my knees, hugging Shorty to my neck. "Do something grand, Bub. Like Geronimo would do."

"We'll see, Sissy, we'll see." Bub lay back on his quilt, put his hands together, and practiced the lonely call of the Mourning Dove. "Oowoo-woo-woo-woo. Oowoo-woo-woo-woo."

On April 9, 1998, I checked into a motel in Orem, Utah after finishing two book signings. I'd just slipped into sweats to relax before calling home to check my answering machine.

For some unexplained reason, my machine wouldn't allow me to retrieve my messages. I called my neighbor on Blue Mountain to see if she'd walk across the road, get my messages, then call me back.

I waited a long time in the room. When the phone rang and I answered, it was my son's voice.

"Mom, I hate to have to tell you this ..." Scott sounded upset and I knew immediately something was wrong.

"What is it?"

"It's bad news, Mom. Real bad. Uncle John ... he ... John Phillip is dead. They found him this morning at his home in Pasco, Washington."

The room around me turned gray. I hadn't seen my older brother in eight years.

One month later, May 9th, 1998, we held a brief memorial service for Bub near my home on Blue Mountain in Colorado. We played the Indian drum and flute. Rain started pelting as Scott sang "Amazing Grace."

My mind went back forty years to that October evening on the creek when Bub and I discussed death.

"I'll make sure you know I'm OK."

"Do something grand, Bub. Like Geronimo would do."

"We'll see, Sissy, we'll see."

I began to tremble when I realized it was my brother's ashes traveling out on the rising wind. An Indian yell erupted from my throat and wailed out from the deepest crevasse of my pain.

Thunder cracked the stillness and lightning jutted across the sky in front of us. Then, a silent calm settled over the mountains and from the distance came the vivid cry of a Mourning Dove. "Oowoo-woo-woo-woo Oowoo-woo-woo-woo."

About the Author

Photograph by Jannis

Lou Dean grew up in Osage County Oklahoma in the era of the one-room schoolhouse and the two-hole outhouse. She graduated from Ponca City High School and attended Oklahoma State University. Her work has appeared in more than fifty magazines during her career as a freelance writer. Her award-winning first book, *Angels in Disguise,* has created a new reality about animals and the part they play in our lives.

A teacher and speaker, Lou Dean now lives on Blue Mountain near Dinosaur, Colorado where she loves to explore the hills with her Jackass, Jesse James, and her Border Collie dogs.

Other books by the author

Angels in Disguise

Paw Prints in My Soul

To order, call:

1-800-521-9221

Or write:

Lou Dean
Clinescot Publishing
Blue Mountain Road
Dinosaur, CO 81610